FLOORWORKS

FLOORWORKS

BRINGING ROOMS TO LIFE
WITH SURFACE DESIGN AND DECORATION

AKIKO BUSCH

LONGMEADOW
PRESS

FLOORWORKS

A RUNNING HEADS BOOK

The following are Registered Trademarks with The U.S. Patent and Trademark
Office: Corian®, Colorcore®, and Formica®.

Published by Longmeadow Press, 201 High Ridge Road, Stamford, Connecticut
06904. No part of this book may be reproduced or used in any form or by any
means, electronic or mechanical, including photocopying, recording, or by
any information storage and retrieval system, without permission in writing
from the publisher.

FLOORWORKS
was conceived and produced by
Running Heads Incorporated
55 West 21 Street
New York, NY 10010

Editor: Jill Herbers
Designer: Stephanie Bart-Horvath
Photo Researcher: Joan Vos
Original Artwork: Michael Horvath
Production Associate: Belinda Hellinger

Library of Congress Cataloging-in-Publication Data

Busch, Akiko.
Floorworks : bringing rooms to life with surface design and
decoration / by Akiko Busch.
p.   cm.
Originally published: Toronto : New York : Bantam Books, 1988.
Includes index.
ISBN 0-681-41591-6
1. Flooring.   2. Floor coverings.   I. Title.
TH2525.B87   1992
690'.16—dc20   92-9711
                                                         CIP

Typeset by Nassau Typographers
Color separations by Hong Kong Scanner Craft Company Ltd.
Printed and bound by C & C Offset Printing Co., Ltd.
0 9 8 7 6 5 4 3 2 1

DEDICATION

To the memory of Mary Smart Busch

ACKNOWLEDGEMENTS

My thanks first and foremost to the craftsmen, artists, designers, and architects who have contributed so greatly to this book. Their willingness to share their work despite demanding schedules and work loads is continuing testimony of their creativity and generosity of spirit.

I am grateful as well to the photographers whose work is shown here. They were unstinting in their own submissions and suggestions of projects I may never have found otherwise. Coleen O'Shea and Becky Cabaza of Bantam Books should also be thanked.

Finally, my thanks to Marta Hallett, Ellen Milionis, and Jill Herbers of Running Heads Incorporated who have been excited by this book from start to finish, and whose excitement has worked as constant, generous, and vital support and encouragement.

CONTENTS

FOREWORD

In a color photograph of the Parthenon, a picture of a masterpiece that itself is a masterpiece, the eight Doric columns that form one end of the temple stand out in relief against a brooding gray sky. Reflections of these columns shimmer across the marble floor, still wet from a sudden rain. The water runoff accentuates the ruts and ridges in the worn surface and the separations that exist between the large marble squares. What the camera lens captured beyond these rich images is the wonder of a still-standing 2,500-year-old surface that bears both the character of antiquity and the punishment of history. The Parthenon's floor is an expression of the skills of ancient artisans who shaped the stones quarried from the nearby mountainside, ground and polished them, and placed them in a setting that reflects the crude technology but incredible vision of an age that saw the birth of Western culture as we know it.

The Romans refined this technology. The baths, basilicas and palaces they built throughout the Empire reflect the skill and confidence they brought to bear when working with decorative materials. By the third century A.D. they could create tile floors whose patterns played tricks on the eye, or formed dazzling landscapes in color, detail and composition: mosaic masterpieces no one would dare set foot on today. Their beauty is based not only on the Roman mastery of technology but also on the fact that they have survived the wars, the cataclysms, the pestilence and the perseverance of civilization in all the intervening centuries. Thus they can be considered miraculous fusions of art with craft and history. To see these surviving floors, even in photographs, is to experience art as it was lived with and used in antiquity, making these floors no less beautiful to walk on than to behold.

Compare these images, if you will, with what fantasy-seeking movie audiences of the 1930s experienced sitting in passive thrall as Fred Astaire whirled Ginger Rogers across the splendid ballrooms of Depression-era musicals. The dancers' footwork was so precise, so flawless thus so dazzling, that they seemed almost not to touch the floor. And the floors in each of these intentionally awesome settings were the ultimate in 20th-century refinement. Bakelite — an early form of plastic — was painted with sunbursts or starbursts and polished to a reflective sheen. The surfaces were so delicate that they remained covered with cardboard until the moment the camera was ready to roll.

Dancing cheek to cheek and toe to toe across those sleek, mirror-bright surfaces, Astaire and Rogers enlivened the aura of glamour and chic that persists in the shiny floors aspired to by so many homemakers. TV commercials have fanned these aspirations, promoting polishes that are ever easier to apply and increasingly more effective in creating surfaces that exceed mere shininess. Flooring manufacturers have followed suit, fabricating products with built-in sheen, their beauty and perfection supplied not by elbow grease but by technology. The sum and substance of this technology has been to advance the idea of floors as pristine surfaces, defiant of wear and use — no heel marks, no nicks from fallen crockery, no stains from spilled food — unlike the floors of antiquity wherein the signs of wear compound their beauty.

Between the two extremes — floors whose surfaces reflect both history and art, and floors that resist the impact of time — lie a vast array of latter-day considerations that are pursued in detail in this book. For floors remain perennial concerns to the architects, designers and craftsmen who fashion them, and to the people who use them daily in their homes, offices, schools and churches.

"The floor is a primary surface in every building I design," says Lester Walker, an architect in Woodstock, New York. "You're always conscious of the floor because you're always touching it. Walking on it, you may not be aware that you're stepping on a particular texture, pattern or color, but you do react subliminally. It affects your reaction to the space you're in.

"I give important consideration to floors at two points in the design process: In the earliest stages when I'm trying to make a client understand the relationship of one volume of space to another, I use floors as a bridge. Later, near the end of the process when the client and I are discussing finish materials, the need for color, pattern and texture dictates the flooring surfaces I specify.

"Of course, when I'm actually conceiving a design, I have particular images in mind. I picture myself walking into the house and being in its handsome foyer, for example, and I try to imagine how it would look and feel to stand there. Although my concerns at this point are focused primarily on volume — six-sided space — I think about what the floor might be, and how to make it express the mood I hope to project."

Carolyn Guttilla, an interior designer in Locust Valley, New York, says, "Floors seem to expand space or reduce it, depending on how you treat them. They are an architectural enhancement that can alter the look and mood of a space dramatically. Because people feel strongly about what they walk on, floors are among my first concerns as a designer.

"You don't have to have large spaces to make a statement, and you don't have to worry about the perishability of creating a *faux-marbre* surface or some other kind of painterly look, for example. The clear sealers we have today will protect painted surfaces indefinitely."

Thanks to technological advances, the various architectural and decorating enhancements conceived for floors over time can now be replicated — in tile, brick, stone, wood or vinyl, and in any of a series of paint applications. How much enhancement we choose is left to our individual taste and discretion.

Less decorative approaches to floor design were advanced by two different schools of thought earlier in the century. California architects Charles and Henry Greene celebrated the floor as a platform for displaying the raw beauty of the shape, color and graining of wood. Although their architecture bore influences of the Arts and Crafts Movement that reached our shores from England, their particular reverence for wood was born of their respect for Japanese architecture, which exalted the material through broad, sweeping roofs, through exposed beams extending beyond the walls themselves, and for its purity as a surface to walk on — even with stockinged feet.

The essence of a Greene & Greene design could be found in the brothers' refinement without violation or decoration of elements found in nature. For Frank Lloyd Wright the use of natural elements was the result of his desire to simulate or extend nature. Like his mentor, Louis Sullivan, Wright chose materials whose colors and textures recalled the natural environment. His most famous house, Fallingwater, was so brilliantly cantilevered over the stream and waterfalls of Bear Run, Pennsylvania, that it is sometimes difficult even now to pinpoint exactly where the natural site ends and the house begins. To underscore this fusion of nature and artifice, he created massive horizontal planes that sustain the rhythm of the house's sandstone terracing.

"Most of the floors in the house are of stone quarried from a site no more than 200 yards away," recalls Edgar Tafel, a longtime Wright apprentice and one of two project architects assigned to Fallingwater. "The floors appear to imitate the rock ledges on which the house was built, though these so-called natural stones were carefully ground, polished and coated with sealer." A number of boulders had to be removed so the house could be built, but Wright allowed one of them

to remain in place. It penetrates the floor to form a "natural" architectural element inside, heightening the mood established by the stone surfaces.

Tafel also recalls designing a house in stages for a man of somewhat limited means: "He built when and as he could — that was how we agreed to work. The house was in a New York suburb, and he asked me to design a system of radiant heating for it: pipes recessed beneath a wood platform surfaced in heat-conducting tiles. That was the goal anyway. All I did at first was create a frame for the system, but instead of laying pipes for heating, the owner brought in sand. He and his family walked on sand until he could afford the flooring — and the heating installation — he wanted. The kids loved it!"

"When it comes to floors for the rooms we live in, there are two things I insist on: They must lie down, and they must be quiet." So wrote the master decorator of the 1950s in *Billy Baldwin Decorates*. "A floor should never jump up at you to the point where people walk around looking at their feet. A floor may be brilliant, but the rest of the room must compensate so the floor is not noticed to the exclusion of everything else."

In a studio in the Tribeca community of Lower Manhattan, Augustus Goertz III, a young artist, looks down at the thickly paint-spattered surface under his feet. "It's become too intense," he says, "too distracting when people come to see my work. I've painted it over many times and I'll have to do it again." Coat upon coat of spilled and dripped paint have given this floor special color richness and texture.

"What appeals to me about it is the structure," says the artist. "There are layers of romanticism and expressionism superimposed on the rigid geometry of parallel lines — an abstract painting applied to the formal logic of the floorboards. My studio floor was an accident, but I can envision the floors in a living space being painted this way. Of course, if I were to create a surface like this deliberately, it would look more planned, more uniformly finished. The point is, whether the floor is deliberate or accidental, I am excited by the idea of standing *on* and *in* the painting."

Perhaps without realizing it, Goertz has explained the enduring brilliance of some of history's most beautiful floors: They succeed because of their artistry, their craftsmanship, their conception, their contribution to a total design scheme, and also because their function is encouraged rather than denied. Their primary purpose, still and always, is to be walked on.

Mervyn Kaufman

INTRODUCTION

The revitalized attention given to decoration in architecture and design has left no surface untouched. Freed from the boundaries of modernism, which did not allow much ornamentation, designers and artists are creating and crafting designs with vitality in color, texture, and pattern. The ongoing human taste for ornament, which ebbs and flows through the centuries, has reappeared with liveliness and wit. This visual exuberance that is the hallmark of contemporary design has spread even to the austere bastions of corporate architecture, which have been invaded by oversize murals, modern tapestries and wallhangings, and immense handpainted tile installations.

The use of such decorating styles in the home is even more widespread, and along with the renewed interest in ornamentation comes a revival in the practice of age-old decorative traditions. The use of stenciling, painted finishes such as trompe l'oeil and faux treatments, wallpaper, wallhangings, architectural ceramics, and decorative glass is being revived with renewed ornamental vigor in home design. Although these treatments all have impressive historical precedents, they are being given contemporary interpretations that result in striking meldings of old and new.

It is with surface design that some of the most austere and neglected areas are brought to life with the application of decorative elements. It is a testament to the strength of this new decorative movement that floors, long considered a background that should recede as much as possible, are now receiving an enormous amount of attention.

What is refreshing about contemporary surface design is that no one particular treatment can be considered most correct. This is a departure from the modernist view, which espoused the integrity of unadorned materials. Frank Lloyd Wright, for example, maintained that if a surface was painted, it suggested that the correct material had not been used in the first place. Contemporary design is diverse, and perhaps what most distinguishes it is that surface decoration is no longer burdened by such dogma. A stenciled or painted finish is not necessarily a decorative afterthought, for example, but rather is intrinsic to the overall design. The simple beauty of wood floors, however, are just as appreciated in the contemporary arts. Each treatment is judged on its own merits, rather than by what qualifications it fulfills for a present movement or popular style.

Whether it is a Tuscan landscape or an abstract application of paint, thread, or tile, this kind of surface design delights the eye so much that we tend to think of it as being purely visual. Our perceptions of the environment, however, are more than purely visual, and it is often what is at our feet that makes this fact most clear. It is not only how our floors look, but how they feel that is integral to our comfort and sense of ease. While these surfaces may be visually appealing, they are also what we stand on, walk across, and play on. We have a tactile connection with floors.

We often experience our environment through the soles of our feet. Whether it is the hot sand of the beach, the cool, wet grass of early morning; or the scorching pavement of the city, these sensations shape our impressions of the environment. And if our perceptions of the world outdoors can be formed by such tactile impressions, so can our perceptions of the world indoors. Often people take their shoes off when they are home. Being barefoot can be a sign of being safe, comfortable, and at ease. Leaving one's shoes at the door is a way of leaving the outside world exactly that — outside.

Our interest in the look and feel of floors may have psychological roots as well. It is, after all, the place where many of us spent a great deal of time as infants and young children, crawling, tumbling, playing, and imagining. Because children view the world from such a limited height, most of the landscape for them is taken up by the floor. The floor was the backdrop for much of our creative activity as children. Whether it was the gigantic checkerboard black-and-white tiles of a grandparent's kitchen or the rich palette and texture of an Oriental carpet, these early impressions often surface in our later design decisions. The values we look for in our environment as adults are often influenced by the spaces which were significant to us as children.

By affecting our perceptions of space, floor surfaces affect the way we use that space. In the wide open loft spaces that are being converted in many cities, it is often the change in floor material rather than in walls that separates one area from another, one "room" from another. Carpeting, wood, and ceramic tiles can all be used in a single loft, but each may be conducive to very different activities.

When deciding which surface material to use on the floor, it is wise to keep in mind that general observations *can* be made and that universal rules *do* apply. While matters of design and decoration, which are purely visual, may rest on highly individual choices and the

vagueries of personal taste, those that have to do with more practical and tangible effects are more concrete. Tile, for instance, may be the ideal choice for a kitchen floor because it is easy to clean and maintain. But it may not be the right selection for a living room floor; because it may be cold to the feet, and sometimes noisy as well, it does not often encourage gatherings. People will be more likely to group where there is a warmer surface, such as a carpeted or wood floor.

It is exciting that the visual vitality and creativity that is found elsewhere in the decorative arts is now being translated to floors, but architects and designers must keep practicality in mind as well. Faux marble floors, for example, do not simply delight the eye with their naturalistic colors and veining, but the wood surfaces they are painted on tend to be warmer and more resilient than their stone counterparts. However, their longevity may be somewhat less than real marble floors. All these considerations must be weighed when laying or designing floors, and it must be remembered who these floors are meant to serve, how, and how often.

Shown here are some of the various decorating traditions, translated into contemporary styles, found on the world at our feet. Some are architectural surface materials, such as natural wood floors; others are applied with paint, stain, or any number of other materials. But whatever the treatment, whether it is a floor stained with dark mahogany polish or a surface that has been spattered with bright paints, vitality in surface design is now an important element to the room itself.

Surface design does not need to be at odds with structure, as was often the case in the past. Now it works with it to enhance the value, architectural sense, and shape of a room. Borders on painted rugs and floorcloths echo and outline the room's shape, bringing a value to the whole. Wood is inlaid in geometric patterns that complement the geometry of the room and the way the viewer approaches it. Architecture and surface design are not only in harmony in the contemporary arts; they work to complement one another. This is the case made, with visual wit, grace, and clarity, by the floors shown in this book.

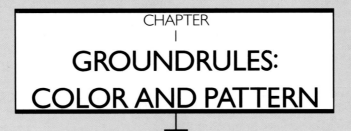

CHAPTER
I
GROUNDRULES:
COLOR AND PATTERN

The power of pattern and color to set the tone of a room is beautifully displayed in this floor design from a house in Malibu. The floor is fashioned from linoleum, but the innovative design gives the mundane material a surprisingly elegant effect.

Architectural designer Nancy M. Pope has used one-and-a-half-inch strips of onyx and travertine — a type of limestone — as well as tiles of solid travertine strips to pattern the floor of an apartment foyer. The striped border corresponds to the stepped progression of the wall at the doorway, bringing out the shape of the foyer.

The floor is often the largest single expanse in an interior, and its design function has been thought of as a backdrop, a subtle background against which other visual activity in the room may occur. Therefore conventional wisdom has held that the motifs, colors, and patterning used in floor design should be subtle and unobtrusive, and should recede into the room.

However, the floor is taking on a more expanded meaning in contemporary design schemes. For as long as designers have been conforming to design conventions, they have been dismissing them as well. In doing so, they have proved that the same visual excitement and intensity that is found on other surfaces, such as walls, can enliven floor design. There are notable historical precedents for floor decoration, such as ornate mosaics of Pompeian architecture in the A.D. first century. Mosaics in black and white or more brightly colored marbles revealed entire narratives, showed elaborate geometric patterns, spelled out inscriptions, and scattered trompe l'oeil objects — painted illusions of real scenes — artfully and actively across the floor. So designers who choose to ignore the convention of the flat and unobtrusive floor have ample historical backup if they execute their work with like wit, thought, and creativity.

Generally, however, when floors *have* been decorated, their design has been dominated by convention. Whether it is the application of color or pattern, floor design has a system of tradition that reinforces our natural perceptions. But it is often by challenging these perceptions that the most intriguing and memorable floors are created. Nature conditions us, for example, to expect specific color progressions in exterior, as well as interior, landscapes. Earth tones

Architect Michael Graves used base, middle, and head color palettes for this area that deviate from the classical norm. Usually browns, grays, and earth colors signal the base; roses, pinks, greens, and yellows indicate the middle; and blue is the head color. But here squares of blue vinyl tile turn the traditional palette upside down. The tiles are meant to suggest light falling onto the floor through square windows. Also notable is the change in floor material to mark different rooms. It is the switch from vinyl to wood on the floor, rather than solid walls, that indicates the shift from the kitchen to the dining area.

Architect Steven Holl has used blocks of white Carrara marble for the floor of a foyer in a New York City apartment. Cut into the marble surface is the delicate outline of a large circle, filled with black grout and marking the center point of entry in the foyer. Beyond is a cork floor and a carpet designed by Holl with the linear motifs carried over from the dining area.

such as greens, browns, and blacks are dark; foliage is usually a middle green tone; and the sky is a lighter blue. Thus we expect a dark value beneath our feet, medium values around us, and the lightest values above. And indeed, most traditionally designed interiors tend to conform to these standards. But by reversing color, twisting it, and otherwise playing with it, powerful and provocative visual statements can be created that artfully challenge and manipulate preconceptions of the environment. Yet, while architects and designers can choose to deviate from such classical color progressions, before dismissing them entirely they must at least recognize that they exist.

It is true that dramatic patterning on the floor, in which motifs are in great contrast to their backgrounds, can create the illusion of a three-dimensional surface which may be jarring and confusing. But subtle floors can also be created, and the design of floors in any part of a house need not be loud or obtrusive to make a statement.

Perceptions of space are also influenced by perceptions of color. Warm oranges and reds on the floor will diminish the apparent size of larger rooms, while cooler greens, blues, and lilacs, as they recede, will make the room appear more spacious.

In applying patterns to the floor, conventional design strategy dictates that the scale of patterns match those found elsewhere in the interior. While actually using the same patterns throughout the room

may indeed be excessive and visually monotonous, a rug with small detailed patterning might be selected because it is similar in dimension to that found on the upholstery in the room. Such formulas, however, are no longer observed with the same fervor by decorators today. Indeed, large bold patterns can happily coexist with smaller, more detailed designs, if there is a likeness in form or color tone. Or it can as well be the *difference* in these elements that makes for visual interest. It can be the contrast in color, tone, or scale that provokes a new, more unique aesthetic. Provocative and innovative design is the result not of following previously established rules but of questioning them and playing with the answers.

There are as many ways of breaking decorating and design rules as there are rules, and the most interesting floors often acknowledge this fact. Color and pattern on the floor *can* continue to serve their traditional functions. The colors in a patterned rug, for instance, may work simply to unite the colors found elsewhere in the interior. But floor design doesn't have to be limited by this conventional approach, and the patterning and color found underfoot may be used for more independent visual expression. Designers have a wealth of tradition to draw on and to explore. That they may either adhere to it or deviate from that tradition renders floor design an area of enormous creative investigation and innovation.

The dotted, luminescent carpeting in this coffee bar is juxtaposed with a wall designed with equal vitality and imagination. The patterns, colors, and textures shown here display how important a role floors can take in setting the tone of a room.

Designers at A2Z have composed a contemporary geometric floor design with pieces of vintage linoleum tile. While the actual pattern is clearly contemporary, the familiar color schemes and chrome dinette set evoke the fifties. Dubbed "Porta-Floor," the linoleum is edged in oak, and though cumbersome, can be removed and reinstalled.

OKG Architects installed sheets of standard, commercial black linoleum with a subtle marbleized pattern on the floor of a residence in Malibu. Strips of blue linoleum serve as a border, emphasizing entry and dividing walls. The steps and platforms are outlined with aluminum strips, which gives them a sculptural air.

CHAPTER
2
WOOD FLOORS

This entryway demonstrates how elaborately patterned floors can be showcased in small foyers. Bird's eye maple squares have been inlaid in long, reddish strips of Honduras mahogany against a background of cherry. The border is walnut with accents of bird's eye maple. Once inlaid, the entire floor was stained a medium brown. The stain was then removed from the square inlays for a nearly electric "jump." Viewed from all angles and heights of a three-story atrium, the floor is a strong example of the dramatic patterning that can be created through wood inlays. It was designed and inlaid by Randy Yost.

Patterns of squares across a dining-room floor have been stained a rich brown, left. The lighter squares and circles retain the paler hues of the natural oak, and display more clearly the natural patterns of the wood's grain. The private residence was designed by architect I. W. Colburn.

Designer Richard Gillette stained an oak floor which leads to an elegant living room a deep mahogany, right. The circular medallion is based on a design by the eighteenth-century English architect Robert Adam and had been masked out prior to staining to remain the color of the original oak floor.

Along with stone, wood is the oldest architectural material known to man. It is an obvious choice for floors, as it is extremely durable and relatively easy to install and maintain. Hardwood planks, for example, are commonly used, as they need comparatively little finish work.

But wood has great aesthetic advantages as well as practical ones. There are few synthetic materials that have the tactile and visual wealth of a wood surface. It is a natural material that often brings with it a warm, organic quality that is all the more welcome in an age when design often appears to be dominated by industrial materials. The textures, values, and hues of its grains all bring forth a refreshing point of contact with the natural world. The patterning and texture found in natural wood grain, moreover, can be as ornate as those created by hand in other materials.

Along with its other many advantages, wood is remarkably versatile. For although it is appreciated most as a natural surfacing material, it can also have beautiful decorative applications that almost transform the quality of the material by manipulating the wood grains. Wood surfaces can be stained, painted, bleached, pickled, inlaid, or decoratively altered in any number of ways.

Stains are the most traditional of wood treatments, and stained wood floors are akin to natural wood floors. Whether it is a cherry floor stained to enhance natural red tones or an oak floor stained with a spectrum of richer hues from deeper reds and auburns to brown, stains work to bring out, highlight, and otherwise enliven the innate hues and textures of the natural material. They can also be used to manipulate wood because they can be applied in such a way as to either enhance and call attention to natural grains or to soften and conceal them.

Stains are best selected in consideration of how different woods absorb them. Pine, because it is a softwood, absorbs stain extremely unevenly; therefore, light gold stains that are close to its real color or a natural finish suit it best. Oak floors, on the other hand, are hardwoods

The enduring value of the wood floor is shown beautifully in both an old-fashioned setting, below, and in heightening the elegance of a contemporary dwelling.

and can take any stain. Red oak will always have a warm, rosy tinge, so stains should be applied that will complement or bring out that color. White oak is more neutral and can take any color. Maple, with an even denser grain and relatively few pores, can absorb very little stain, so again, a natural finish is most suitable for it. Because it is among the hardest woods, maple is used for areas of heaviest traffic, such as gyms and stages where decorative staining may not be top priority.

There are many other treatments as well. Traditional oak floors can be scrubbed with an ordinary bleach solution, then rinsed and sealed with polyurethane for a pale, shimmering effect that will highlight the patterns of their grains. Pickling, on the other hand, is a process that works to subdue the natural hues and textures of wood grain, resulting in an even, polished look. Solutions such as lime and water or gesso and paint are applied to sanded, unfinished, open-grained wood surfaces and are absorbed by the wood's fiber at different speeds. The pigment is applied, let to stand for 20 to 60 minutes, and is then wiped clean. Grain patterns recede according to the varying absorption rates. Opacity is determined by the length of time the pigment remains on the surface before being wiped clean.

Wood floors can make an office space much more personal and inviting, as shown in these two patterned examples. Heery Interiors designed this custom ash and walnut surface, above, for an office in Atlanta. The maple and walnut floor, right, was custom designed by Susan Kennedy.

A heavy gray wash was applied to this floor to make a striking pattern that works both to bring out the beauty of the light-toned wood and create an interesting visual focus to the room.

The striking beauty of red oak is seen from a top view, opposite page, showing patterns and shapes that can be made with hardwood. The floor was designed by Susan Shacket.

The traditional properties of wood are mixed with a contemporary pattern to create an altogether refreshing surface, right. Designed by Suzan Santiago, the floor is made of Walnut Brittany.

Wood grains can be manipulated to even greater decorative extremes in inlaid surfaces. Wood inlay evolved as a decorative art throughout Classical and Medieval periods, reaching its height in the Italian Renaissance when its patterns represented heraldic designs, mythological figures, even entire allegories. Veneers in woods of contrasting grains and hues were cut into pieces and matched, glued, and applied to heavier panels.

Patterned parquet floors are, of course, the most expansive applications of inlays, and the elegance in this tradition has continued in contemporary design. While Italian parquet floors tended to suggest the inexact mottles and streaks of marble slabs, French and German artisans closely observed the properties of the wood itself and enhanced them. Their designs were more geometric, with architectural patterning that tended to be more visually complementary to the lines of the room or building they were in. Contemporary artisans draw on both of these decorative traditions.

Similarly, marquetry can be applied to the floor in more intricate designs. A process in which different woods, and sometimes ivory, are fitted together and glued to a common background, marquetry can create more finely detailed designs and pictures. It is often used to depict a specific symbol or image — the tree of life, for instance, or a symbol of the zodiac.

Inlaid wood floors can serve any number of purposes; the variety in their patterns and textures answer to the variety of their

The red oak used for this floor, left has a hand-hewn primitive look to it that has been achieved first by painting the floor black, and then sanding most of the paint away. The result is a surface that appears worn and aged. Designed by Randy Yost, the floor is punctuated with commercial blue ceramic tiles.

Mother-of-pearl inlays blossom from a white maple vine in the border detail by Randy Yost, below. The dark background is ibi and the lighter accent, cherry. The red oak basket weave and cherry background have been stained in a pale bisque. Yost used the floral and vine accent on the border sparingly, thereby giving it an even more dramatic effect.

applications. Generally speaking, high traffic areas such as kitchens and hallways are best treated in light woods that conceal dirt and scratches better than darker woods. Likewise, high-contrast patterns will distract the eye from surfaces marred by dust, debris, and scratches, the results of normal wear and tear. The weave of a basket pattern, for example, will draw the eye across the surface rather than allow it to be distracted by imperfections. Finally, soft lustre finishes are easier to maintain than high lustres and also show less evidence of use.

The rich patterns of wood floors can be subtle or more electric. In determining pattern and material, it is important to consider the patterning elsewhere in the room. Small entryways are often ideal for elaborate wood floors as there may be little for the eye to observe but the floor. For a living area, on the other hand, with patterned textiles and upholstery, a more subtle floor design might be appropriate.

One of the beauties of applying geometric patterns at floor level is that their designs will shift as the eye moves. The designs that lie at our feet do not remain static. As they are viewed from different angles, perspectives may change, making for a moving, fluid pattern. Squares become diamonds, and vertical stripes become diagonals. The use of different woods — walnut, maple, cherry, or oak, for example — and their varieties of texture and color can yield extravagant landscapes in wood.

But it is not simply the patterning that shifts as the eye moves. Often, the grain of the wood will have a luminescence to it, and it will catch light much like a sheet of iridescent silk. The tone and hue of its colors will depend entirely upon how the wood has been positioned on the floor and from what angle it is viewed.

Despite these ornate patterns, wood floors remain utilitarian surface above all, designed to accommodate heavy traffic. They are as practical as they are visually rewarding.

Inlaid green marble was combined with ibi to create a startling pattern of contrasts in material, color, and texture. The floor was designed by Randy Yost.

A rich combination of different woods and various stains, left, create a colorful and intricately patterned floor.

Although the quartered oak and walnut pattern installed here by Kentucky Wood Floors, opposite page, graces none other than the Oval Office at the White House, the elegant diagonal stripes would be as applicable to the somewhat less grand maneuverings, negotiations, and meetings that occur in most other houses.

Synthetic finishes, of course, add to the durability of wood surfaces, and contemporary wood floors enjoy the advantages of recently developed varnishes and finishes that make them more damage-resistant than their predecessors. A polyurethane finish permits wood to withstand excessive traffic and use, and when reapplied from time to time, will render a wood floor highly resistant to wear and tear without noticeable effect on its natural color. Excessive layers of polyurethane and oil, however, will darken the surface, so professional floor finishers often use a clear nonyellowing varnish with an alcohol, toluene or aliphatic-resin base. Acrylic finishes also make for a permanent abrasion-resistant surface that does not need waxing.

Contemporary wood floors sometimes have the further advantage of portability. One recent European "floating" system permits the installation of prefinished strips, planks, or parquet squares without nails or adhesive. The pieces can be taken up and reinstalled later at a different location.

As is clear on these pages, the appeal of wood floors has not diminished in the least at a time when the experimentation and use of synthetic materials has been promoted. The organic beauty, warmth, and spirit of wood surfaces, their ability to be transformed, and their capacity for rich, decorative patterning, continue to offer an appealing, and often arresting, alternative to a floor surface created from more modern materials.

The herringbone oak pattern of a hallway has been designed and inlaid by Kentucky Wood Floors, right. Both the shift in patterning and the inlaid border work to separate the hall area from adjacent rooms, despite the fact that the same material has been used in both.

The star pattern in the "Citation" design, by Kentucky Wood Floors, opposite page, has been formed by plain walnut with jade centers. Each is framed by oak pickets. Such patterns in wood tend to be fluid, changing as they are viewed from different angles and in different lights.

CHAPTER
3
PAINTED AND STAINED FLOORS

This handpainted area "rug" has been applied to the concrete floor of a hallway by Tim Street-Porter and Annie Kelly. Underneath the pattern, the floor was painted a high-gloss gray. While painted area "rugs" are themselves a tradition in the decorative arts, the pale colors and abstract geometric design used here give the art a more contemporary look.

The painted floor was commonplace in Colonial America. Flat blues, greens, reds, and terra-cottas, with stenciled or handpainted patterns and borders, often embellished the plank floors common to that period. For the past several decades, however, the notion of painting "over" the organic texture and grain of wood has been akin to a criminal act. At long last, painted floors are again finding acceptance. While the natural wood floors that found such favor in modern design because of their simplicity have not lost their appeal, it is now considered appropriate to paint them as well. In fact, it appears that a small moment of decorative history is repeating itself with the renewed enchantment of the painted floor.

Floors have been painted for several reasons through the history of the decorative arts. Like wood furniture, wood floors were often covered with paint in an effort to conceal low-grade materials or, sometimes, shoddy craftsmanship. A coat of paint or surface patterning not only delighted the eye, but also distracted it from worn boards, knots in the planks, or inexpert construction.

Painted floors were also an obvious alternative to costlier area rugs and textiles. Imitations of area rugs were painted on the floor as surrogates for their textile counterparts, and like them, helped to focus attention on a defined area. A painted runner, for example, drew the eye down a hallway, while an area rug in a dining room acted as a visual focus for that space. Such designs were obviously unable to offer the texture and surface richness of rugs and carpets. What they may have offered instead was a delicacy, a fragility in design.

The hall runner painted by Leslie Ann Powers, far left, was inspired by an antique Chinese Ming Dynasty carpet. The carpet, however, was square, so Powers adapted her designs and motif to the narrow, rectangular hallway. While the outside border is an exact recreation of the carpet's border, the motifs of the interior were applied in a new composition that conforms to the long, narrow confines of the runner. Each element itself, however, remains as it was on the original carpet.

This grided floor, left, was created and airbrushed by Serpentine Studio. The grid was handpainted with a metallic copper paint.

The painted floor "rug," right, designed by Nicholas Calder for a hallway and painted by Rinder's New York Flooring, combines painted, stained, and faux surfaces. The center medallion has been painted with acrylics to suggest it is in relief. Indeed, it appears to be rising off the floor, which has itself been stained a pale taupe. The border, on the other hand, is black faux marble. This is an excellent example of how different materials and styles can converge for an elegant design.

To disguise a badly stained concrete floor, left and above left, OKG Architects spattered flat and metallic paint across its surface. The existing grid of cracks was then filled with black caulking to emphasize the pattern.

The juxtaposition of interesting textures and surfaces play up the warm tones of this kitchen. Interior designer Ronn Jaffe, ASID/IBD, selected three different species of natural wood on the floor: wenge, padauk, and ash laid in a dramatic herringbone pattern. Polished bronze inlays create a border.

The black-and-white border painted by Decorative Arts Limited is in dramatic contrast to the rich brown stains used elsewhere on this oak floor, opposite page. As shown here, the use of paints and stains on a single surface makes an elegant pattern that juxtaposes the flat, stark, painted surfaces with the warm glow of wood grain.

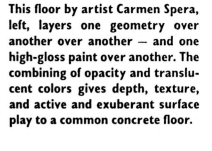

This floor by artist Carmen Spera, left, layers one geometry over another over another — and one high-gloss paint over another. The combining of opacity and translucent colors gives depth, texture, and active and exuberant surface play to a common concrete floor.

Contemporary floors are often painted for rather different reasons. The intent is not to camouflage flaws in materials or workmanship, nor to use painted "rugs" as less costly stand-ins for their textile counterparts. While painted surfaces may, of course, serve such ends, they now exist purely for their own decorative appeal.

Although painted floors may still replicate rugs, they tend to be looser adaptations than their more utilitarian predecessors. Rather than seriously trying to copy elaborately stylized oriental rugs, these designs frequently reflect the aesthetics currently found elsewhere in the visual arts. The expressionist compositions found in contemporary painting and graphics may be used, or more abstract patterning rendered in a post-modern pastel palette may occur. As in previous periods, geometric patterning remains popular, rendered in either freehand or stenciled designs.

Aside from pattern and composition, the effect of such a "rug" can be heightened when its finish differs from that of the immediate area surrounding it. If the unpainted portion of the floor has a matte finish, for example, a high-gloss finish on the "rug" will make the painting stand out all the more. Or, if the "rug" is painted in bright colors on an unpainted wood floor, its impact will be even stronger. In determining the color, finish, and pattern of the painted "rug,"

Designed by Richard Knapple, the geometric pattern for this model room floor and its border have an Art Deco motif. The floor was initially stained a blond tone by Rinder's New York Flooring, then stenciled with an ebony stain.

it is crucial to determine the traffic it will absorb as well as its overall purpose — be it purely ornamental, a directive for traffic flow, or simply a visual focus.

Floor painting need not be limited to designs that echo rugs. Floors can be painted much more extensively, and the finishes available on the market offer a wide variety of options. While earlier painted floors tended to use flat colors, the spectrums, textures and finishes available today allow as many different treatments with paint as there are ideas. Traditional deck paints can be used for thick, dense, high-gloss surfaces or eggshell paints can be used for a softer, matte finish. Acrylic paints can be used over stains for detailed designs, and metallic paints can be used for either a topcoat or an undercoat. Likewise, Zolotone is a recently developed product that achieves the texture of spattered paint directly from the can. Available in many colors, it is especially suited to high-traffic areas because it hides dirt.

Natural wood stains can be used like paint on wood floors to create dramatic patterning. The uses of wood stains here differ from those in the previous chapter in that these use stain for color and pattern. Their purpose is to provoke visual interest rather than simply to enhance the organic texture and graining of the wood. What is

Painters at Serpentine Studio created an apartment with a marine theme for a client transplanted from Miami to New York, left. Stylized ocean images ornament the border of the floor. Here hand-painted marlins fly from gray waves to an orange-colored beach.

Richard Knapple used an indigo blue stain for the floor of an exotic interior, opposite page, that is richly patterned elsewhere with kilim rugs and Indonesian batik. The border pattern of the floor has been stencilled with motifs drawn and enlarged from those found on the batik.

unique about using stains in such a way is that they, by nature, cannot help but do both. This accentuation of wood grains, plus the translucence offered by stains, give floors a decidedly different look than when paints are used for making patterns.

Most artisans will agree that even a design that covers the entire floor area will demand a border both to rule in the design itself, thereby completing the room, and to visually emphasize the shape of the room by echoing it. The contours of all the elements in a room — decorative molding, a fireplace — can be underscored by painted borders that conform to their outlines. Such borders can also work well on their own as decorative accents.

The way that painted and stained floors are created today illustrates the fact that floor design is no longer secondary, nor are its elements necessarily sedate and unobtrusive. Instead, design on these surfaces can be as lively, vibrant, and arresting as design found elsewhere in the interior. And as is amply clear here, paints and stains are no longer used simply to cover, conceal, or camouflage. Rather, through transparent glazes or dense layering, detailed patterning or more spontaneous spattering, matte or high-gloss finishes, they are purposefully used to create lush landscapes.

CHAPTER
4
STENCILED FLOORS

This floor design, which features motifs borrowed from fabric elsewhere about the room, shows that stenciling is not always the simple art it seems, and that patterns can be elaborately applied.

The original purpose of stenciled floors was to recreate the intricate pattern and weave of rugs and carpets with paints and glazes. The intention of stenciling was not to strictly imitate the rugs themselves, as was often the case with painted and stained floors, but to echo the *designs* of the rugs. Geometric and stylized floral patterns were applied with simple cutouts which repeated elaborate designs found on woven textiles. But the softness in color and design that is present in stenciling conveys a delicacy that may be absent in textile counterparts.

Stenciling thrived in American folk art from about 1775 to 1840, since real textiles were too costly for most homes. It developed from overall spattered designs that had a confetti-like effect, to simple geometric patterns rendered in flat colors, and finally to more ornate floral designs that attempted to replicate the elaborate designs found on European area rugs and textiles. Such historic patterns from Colonial America remain available and are especially suited to restorations of houses from this period.

Simple rows of wide flooring planks invited decoration, and stencils were the most practical and efficient means of decorating. Moreover, if a design faded over the course of time, the stencil pattern allowed it to be reapplied easily and quickly. Stenciling also was — and still is — a decorative practice that could be used to conceal flaws in wood floors or inferior craftsmanship, and the stencil patterns were often placed strategically to disguise such defects. But if this was the origin of the art, the stenciled floor has since come to be a less purely practical, imitative practice and has a decorative tradition all its own.

Many stenciled floors continue to use rugs and carpets as their decorative departure point. Aside from being applied to an entire surface, stenciled patterns can also follow the general outline of runners or area rugs. Whether it is the geometrics of Navajo rugs or the stylized natural motifs of Oriental carpets, most rug patterns can be easily transferred by stencils. In these cases, the paints and glazes used in stenciling are nearly transparent; elsewhere, it is the layering

This oak floor, opposite page, was stenciled with standard latex floor paints. Because the color of the oak is part of the overall design, it visually connects the "rug" with the floor, demonstrating one of the unique decorative options of stenciled design.

The charm of stenciling was brought into this living room, left, by painter Lynn Goodpasture.

For an entrance to a house in Connecticut, right, Lynn Goodpasture created a design composed of diagonal bands of a leaf pattern, interrupted by a delicate parade of marching lions, tigers, elephants, peacocks, and the occasional palm tree.

The deep-gray-and-white geometric patterning of this oak floor, opposite page, was created with the same set of stencils as the floor on page 50, but with different configurations. Both floors are by Decorative Arts Limited.

Stenciler Laura Torbet scattered hearts, streamers, and scraps of confetti across a study floor, top right, in a random, spontaneous, and altogether festive arrangement. Although a limited number of images were used, this is not noticeable because of the variety in their arrangement.

The tulip floor designed by Cile Lord and painted by Lynn Goodpasture, bottom right, combines stenciling with handpainting. The floor was initially stained a deep, dark green. Tulip blossoms were then stenciled over the stained surface in white, and the varied colors were applied by hand on the white background. Leaves and ferns were stenciled in lighter green across the darker surface. The contrast in color tones creates an unusually dramatic effect not associated with florals.

A decorated counter and floor border of crowing roosters by painter Lynn Goodpasture brings stenciling into every room.

and gradual building of color that distinguishes the stenciled design. In many ways, this type of stenciling really only plays with the idea of a rug. If the boards of an oak floor remain visible through the pattern or the glaze, the overall design may be provocative and arresting, arousing a curiosity and eagerness to discover what exactly the surface finish is.

Stencil patterns can be designed to represent tile and inlaid wood surfaces as well. Squares, diamonds, hexagonals, triangles, and any number of other geometric configurations created by tiles can be applied by stencils. Geometric shapes can be combined with the less regimented floral or animal forms, which distinguish stenciling from tile work, giving a floor visual variety. Likewise, the checkerboard or herringbone patterns of parquet wood floors can be suggested by stencil. When these designs are rendered in a palette other than that of the expected natural wood tones, they become more provocative and challenging. Contemporary craftsmen and designers tend to take delight in devising such picturesque incongruities — for instance, parquet floors that have been depicted in pastel colors. Stencil patterns that adhere to traditional rigid and rectangular geometric patterns of textiles, tiles, or woods can be given a life of their own with center medallions that use more contemporary motifs. These include pop graphics that feature Campbell soup cans or Chiquita bananas

The oak floor of a bathroom was bleached and then stained white by painter Lynn Goodpasture before she stenciled it, opposite page. While the stencil pattern repeats itself at precise intervals, the placement of the shell motif at intersections is more random. Similarly, each shell has been handpainted uniquely. The combination of precise repetition and spontaneous handpainting is common in contemporary stenciling.

Virginia Crawford created a trellis dot pattern for a small bathroom floor with oil-base paint, left. The repeating dots were stenciled, while the flowers scattered throughout were painted by hand. Two coats of a hard acrylic varethane finish forms a protective coat.

Artists at Decorative Arts Ltd. used simple geometrics and a restrained palette of black and brown, right, for this stencilled stairway runner that provokes visual interest in an otherwise dark and narrow stairway.

The leaves of a crossed garland pattern created and painted by Cile Lord, opposite page, were based on a wreath of leaves around the neck of a maiden in a painting by Botticelli. The garland weaves a diamond pattern across the oak floor, and with the floral patterning elsewhere in the interior, creates a baroque garden.

which attest to the fact that stenciling is a decorative art that lends itself, and indeed brings grace and beauty, to such visual dissonance.

Patterns can be applied across large areas in precise geometric repeats; or they can be more spontaneous and random. Leaves, flowers, scraps of confetti, and martini glasses can all be scattered across the floor with paints and glazes in less mathematical arrangements for a festive, but permanent, effect. It is obvious, then, that contemporary floor stenciling no longer seeks just to recreate, either with subtlety or real precision, the patterning found on carpets and rugs, tiles, and wood. Like the stenciling found on walls, that on floors has acquired its own traditions.

Stenciling also lends itself to border decoration. Often, an ancient Greek-styled key border or a vine or leaf pattern winding along a border can be ornament enough, and can work to emphasize the shape of the room. Checkered borders become a visual accent and are often compatible with tiled surfaces. Or a single stenciled border stripe may be sufficient, especially if the room has a great many patterns in fabrics or upholstery. In that case anything more than a

The floral pattern of John Canning's single stenciled border, opposite page, takes its cues directly from the flowered curtains.

A combination of pickling, marblizing, combing, and stenciling, all by John Canning, together create a delicate floor design, left and above. The stylized floral motif carries on stenciling tradiiton, but the combination of surface painting techniques used here make for a richer, more contemporary surface.

simple border can make for visual clutter. Borders are a decorative way of suggesting boundaries within a space or the separation between two areas in a larger open space. While stenciling for this purpose is purely decorative, and hardly the most practical or sure means to define space, it certainly works as visual reinforcement.

Although such floors may seem slightly more precious than their textile, tile, or wood counterparts, they are actually no less durable. Polyurethane finishes such as varethane, acrylic varnishes, and waxes make stenciled floors impervious to age and wear. Most craftsmen recommend that one or two coats of varnish be reapplied from time to time. This should be sufficient, because the shine and yellowing of multiple layers may ultimately interfere with color and design. The type of protective coating used will affect the visual quality of the finished surface. Glossy varnishes enhance bright colors by making them shine, while matte finishes yield flatter, duller surfaces. In addition these floors are often strengthened by stains and washes.

The real challenge and unique beauty of floor stenciling lies in the way in which the application of design works with the surface of the floor. It is the nature of stenciling that patterns are applied to a surface in such a way that part of the surface remains visible. And it is often *how* the surface remains visible that makes for the greatest visual delight. The grains of a wood floor, its hues, or even its texture can be made to emerge through the decorative patterning in unique ways, often creating provocative images. Whether the surface is brick, stone, terra-cotta or concrete, all of which lend themselves to stenciling, the combination of surface and stencil is bound to be interesting in bringing about lively visual and textural play. Since any surface that has some texture and does *not* have a slippery, waxed finish or high-gloss glaze — such as some ceramic tile — can be stenciled, the varieties are many. The way in which the natural surface and the applied surface work together is often what distinguishes floor stenciling as a decorative art with its own firm and fast traditions.

The pattern on the floor of this child's room is based on a medieval manuscript design. The stenciling was done by John Canning.

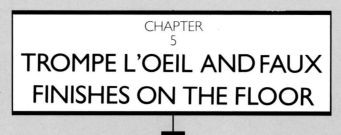

CHAPTER 5
TROMPE L'OEIL AND FAUX FINISHES ON THE FLOOR

*Common plywood flooring was transformed
to what looks like an elaborate terrazzo
surface — small chips of marble set in
cement and then polished — with paints and
glazes, showing the magic of faux finishes.
The floor was designed by Richard Gillette.*

Richard Gillette and Stephen Shadley designed a faux marble floor pattern in pinks, pale greens, and grays. The oversize pattern is based on designs found in the Vatican. The fact that it was applied to a somewhat less majestic and austere environment — the vinyl tile flooring of a showroom — proves that grand painted deceptions can indeed occur anywhere.

For nearly as long as architects and craftsmen have used stone as a building material, they have used the painted finish as its surrogate. With paints and glazes, faux surfaces can be created to duplicate real stones, among them marble, granite, limestone, terrazzo, slate, and serpentine, or to recreate with paint other surfaces, from wood to ceramic tile. The veins of marbles, the burls and grains of wood, the mottled lustre of lapis lazuli, or the precise inlays of ivory can all be visually recreated with the skillful application of gesso and gilt. Tools of the trade, such as paintbrushes, sponges, squeegees, and combs, among others, are used to apply paint and varnish in textures and designs that convincingly evoke an actual stone or marble.

Such finishes are often structurally more practical for buildings incapable of bearing the weight of the real stone. In addition, the installation of a painted floor is often less costly than the inlay or surfacing of real stone or marble. Painted diamond shapes of lapis lazuli are clearly more affordable than inlays of the actual stone. And there is no need to search the quarries of Italy for the right stone when color and veining can be created to specification.

While faux surfaces other than marble can be as easily and as imaginatively devised, it is the delicate color and veining of marble that make it most often emulated. The subtle tones of the stone and its veining can be created to correspond to colors used elsewhere in the interior.

Faux marble can also be rendered in colors that are decidedly not endorsed by nature, making fascinating fantasy marbles. Soft earth tones of a finish in pinks, browns, peaches, or pale greens shot through with electric blue veining, or dense greens and blacks punctuated by peach veins can look surprisingly natural, without bearing the least resemblance to any actual geological palette. The interplay of color and veining can be specified so there are an infinite number of possibilities.

Designers of Decorative Arts Limited applied a border of cream-colored faux marble around an oak floor that had been stained a deep brown. The sharp outlines of the border define the shape of the room and emphasize the fireplace, itself a very real black marble.

Artisans of Tromploy Inc. created a checkerboard of faux marble in a pale orange cream and a pink beige with a light terra-cotta border, left. It occurs in a hallway that connects a bedroom addition to an older Colonial house in Connecticut. The owners felt that a painted floor would be more in keeping with the spirit of the house than actual marble or stone, and specified a checkerboard design, but one rendered in subtle tones rather than those of more dramatic contrasts found in most checkerboard patterns. The compass rose in the center, — rendered in a pure white faux marble — is the focal point of the passageway. Because of the owners' nautical interests, it actually points true north. By doing so, it is slightly off center with the lines of the hallway, heightening its visual interest.

Michael Thornton-Smith created a checkerboard of fantasy marbles in bright pumpkin tones which are more dramatic and exaggerated than those usually found in marble, opposite page. The telephone, also painted, appears to have been carved from a block of lapis lazuli, a new extreme in communications equipment.

Craftsmen at Serpentine Studio used natural sea sponges to transform a parquet wood floor to slabs of solid black granite. Layer upon layer of black, gray, silver, and white paint were applied in irregular patterns by the uneven surfaces of the sponges. Each "slab" is slightly different, adding to the trompe l'oeil illusion of separate blocks of stone.

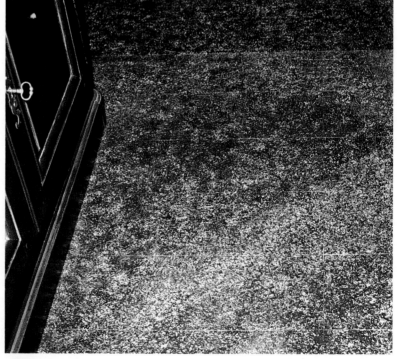

Painter and muralist Thomas Melvin created a faux mosaic floor for the Herman Miller Showroom in Chicago, opposite page. The stylized border and interior motifs have a grand genealogy, based loosely on designs found on a marble mosaic floor in a villa belonging to Hadrian, the second-century Roman emperor.

The owners of a Long Island residence wanted a diamond pattern with square inlays for their entryway, left and above. Polly Lewis, a painter specializing in faux finishes, designed the faux marble pattern in earth tones — ocher with delicate veining — for what was actually an oak floor. Greenish-gray faux serpentine inlays mark the intersections of the stone and the border. Lewis used oil-base paints with a single coat of polyurethane, which should be reapplied every two years.

The granite checkerboard floor designed by architects at A2Z, right, is, in fact, a more resilient and acoustically appealing alternative — vinyl tile.

Slabs of faux marble for a floor designed by Nick Grande were handpainted by Rinder's New York Flooring, right. The wood floor was initially stained a pale taupe, and the delicate veining was added in acrylic. Subdued color and veining form a surface that is neither too lively nor distracting.

A grid of ceramic tiles was recreated by Michael Thornton-Smith for an expansive Manhattan loft, left. Sheets of thick plywood were screwed onto the deteriorated wood floor, and were then sanded and painted to resemble tiles. The painted tiles have a warmer feel than the real thing, weigh much less, and are far less costly.

Whether the faux marble surface replicates a real marble or is a fantasy stone instead, its translucent layering and delicate veining can bring depth and texture to the floor surface. It can do so in a subtle and unobtrusive pattern, or it can be more lush and dramatic. While faux marbles based on real stone tend to be soft, fantasy marbles can be much brighter, almost radiant in color.

Finally, to heighten such mysteries of material, trompe l'oeil, a technique in which paint is used to simulate scenes that fool the eye because they appear to be real, is often employed to create objects that appear to lie atop the faux surface. Scattered and broken crockery, goldfish ponds, wine glasses, and napkins can all find their way as easily to the faux floor as to the real floor. This play with fantasy materials and trompe l'oeil makes these finishes very popular today. Seemingly incongruous colors and textures appeal to the eye, and to the mind as well, and contemporary designers exploit this sense of intrigue. Sky-blue marble floors that appear to have unquestionably genuine veining nevertheless *do* question our perceptions of the material world and appear to be the obvious and picturesque offspring of the natural and synthetic worlds.

But a great appeal of faux stone floors lies in how they achieve the rich hues and delicate tone and veining of the stone without its austere, cold surface. Painted marble walls may be a purely visual delight, but painted marble floors are just as pleasing in a tactile way. They have a softer feel than stone, a resilience and a warmth.

Combing, pickling, and marblizing by John Canning have all made this wood floor in a dining room a splendid fantasy landscape.

The Greek key border and faux bois (wood) diamond pattern were executed by both stenciling and handpainting. The grain of the surface finish is "poetic": it is not meant to replicate any specific wood, but is a looser adaptation of the pattern and texture found in authentic parquet floors. The floor was designed by Evergreene Painting Studios.

A checkerboard floorscape by John Canning combines pickling, combing, and marblizing that together make for extravagent surface design. The border of faux serpentine is an especially lavish touch.

Situated at the base of a short atrium in an interior designed by Booth-Hansen & Associates, the fantasy marble inlay floor is actually concrete that has been painted, varnished, and waxed by painter Thomas Melvin. Viewed through leaves of shrubbery, the patterned stone surface creates the illusion of an Italian garden courtyard.

Not content with the massive faux granite stones they had installed in a New York City apartment foyer, Gary Finkel and Clyde Wachsberger of Tromploy Inc. proceeded to install a small fish pond in it with, naturally, a school of goldfish in somewhat perplexed immobility. The room is designed to look "Pompeian" with crumbling frescoes on the wall and shattered crockery strewn across the floor which has caused visitors to adeptly step aside.

Most painted faux and trompe l'oeil surfaces are on wood (usually oak), and wood offers acoustical advantages over stone. The variance in density in wood grains allows for the material to absorb sound at equally varying rates, thereby softening and muffling sound slightly. Stone, on the other hand, is a denser, harder material and tends to reflect and carry sound more. Objects striking a stone surface make a somewhat clearer, more resonant, and of course, louder sound. So faux finishes not only delight the eye and provoke the mind, they have added appeal to the senses in both a tactile and acoustical way.

In the end, what makes faux stone and trompe l'oeil finishes so desirable for the floor is not how they imitate the real thing, but how they deviate from it. A goldfish pond that is painted is obviously a more feasible venture than one which is real — and one doesn't have to step around it for fear of getting wet. Faux marble floors offer the delicate color and veining of the natural material, yet they also offer a broader and more inventive palette. Faux marble surfaces bring elegance and refinement to an interior just as the real stone does, but the elegance is less precious; it takes itself less seriously. It aims to enchant rather than to impress. Fantasy finishes do not offer the longevity of real stone, but their decorative, tactile, and acoustical benefits offer a picturesque alternative with merits all their own.

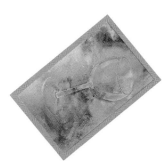

Craftsmen of the Day Studio Workshop created a faux marble surface with intricate inlays for a dining room floor. While the sub-dued tones of the marble appear to be altogether natural, the trompe l'oeil wine glass indicates that this is indeed a fantasy floor where dropped glasses do not necessarily shatter.

Don't blame the cat; it's only trompe l'oeil. This fallen jade plant and faux stone was painted directly on old linoleum tile in a Manhattan kitchen, above. The entire treatment was executed by Tromploy, Inc.

TILED FLOORS

The tile floor designed for Hughes Entertainment by Design Spec Flooring is based on the traditional checkerboard of black-and-white tiles. The grid, however, is punctuated by occasional tiles with lively squiggles, spatters, and other updated graphics that give it a contemporary twist.

What readily comes to mind about the use of architectural ceramics in the history of the decorative arts is its splendor as ornament, its rich geometric patterning, as well as its illustrative narratives, all of which have decorated the surface and structure of architecture in practically all cultures. The application of ceramic tile on the *floor*, however, is a tradition that is based as firmly on pragmatism as on decoration. The inherent durability of ceramic tiles, their fire resistance, and the ease with which they can be maintained have rendered them ideal flooring materials for centuries, and they remain so in contemporary residential design. Ceramic tiles are especially suited to areas of high traffic and areas that have direct access to the outdoors. Both water and steam resistant, tile is an especially obvious flooring candidate for bathrooms and kitchens. It also provides efficient insulation with a capacity both to remain cool in hot climates and to retain heat in colder ones. In homes designed to be energy-efficient, ceramic floor tiles help to absorb and retain the sun's heat, often acting as passive solar collectors.

While the varying qualities of tiled surfaces may distinguish them as an overall practical and sturdy flooring material, floor tiles can be used to architectural and decorative advantage. Tile is appealing for its capacity to shape space, and then to embellish it. A grid of large floor tiles will establish a sense of spaciousness, while the detail implicit in patterns of one-inch tiles are more visually restraining. A horizontal band will give greater width, while vertical bands add length.

A grid of deep gray Italian ceramic tiles by Marazzi is broken by a diamond-shape inset of the same kind of tiles, opposite page. The application demonstrates how tiles can be used in varying configurations to create pattern and visual interest.

Designer Dorothy Davis made blue-and-white square tiles by hand for all the surfaces of a small bath, left. The linear patterns used on the walls is sharply contrasted by the diagonal geometrics of the floor. The design illustrates how standard shapes like squares can be installed in a variety of configurations to create dramatic graphics and patterns.

Dorothy Hafner's handpainted terra-cotta tiles are titled "Asterisks." Installed in an irregular pattern against a ground of blank white tiles, the color and design become all the more effective. As shown here, painted tiles can make a vibrant visual accent when used imaginatively with solids.

Architect Alan Buchsbaum used two sizes and three colors of commercial Italian ceramic tile from Fiandre, left, for a New York City kitchen. Pink, black, and white tiles are arranged in varying patterns — in part geometric and in part more random — to create an innovative design.

Ceramist Dorothy Hafner has constructed a floor piece, titled "Chevron," below, that works as a porcelain carpet. Handpainted porcelain tiles are arranged with blank, white tiles in a seemingly random pattern that alternates between an electric design and pauses of visual calm.

Phillip Maberry's handmade, hand-drawn, and hand-glazed floor tiles, right, demonstrate some of the surface possibilities that become available when traditional tile rules — such as the rectangular shape and the grid format — are removed. Here each tile is a small canvas. Together, they paint an expressionist landscape on the finished surface.

The form of tiles makes them conducive to border accents which are often ample ornament for the floor. Or, a border of glazed and decorated tiles can be used to liven up an expanse of solid tiles. These borders can be made to emphasize the shape of a room or to delineate smaller areas within a larger space.

Tile not only reinforces the shape of space, and our perceptions of it. It is also used to ornament and to embellish, and like wall tiles, floor tiles can be used in three basic ways. A tile may be used as a single decorative unit that accents a solid surface. Tiles may also be used to create a larger pattern. Finally, they may be used as components in a *narrative,* a pictorial mural rendered in tile. Within these groups, though, the decorative options offered here are many. Even identically shaped tiles permit numerous different patterns and configurations. Square tiles can form grids that run perpendicular to the wall, or rows of diamonds that run on a diagonal, or brick patterns on a rectangular plane. When several configurations are used in a single installation, the continuity in material can be juxtaposed by the variety in pattern for a provocative visual effect. Or, the tiles used elsewhere in the interior

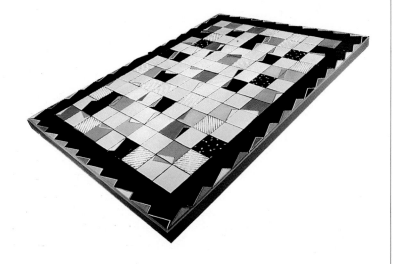

This bedroom floor designed by Alan Buchsbaum shows how commercial tile can be used in a wholly inventive way when placed in the right setting and design.

can be repeated on the floor in a different pattern, making for both aesthetic unity and diversity.

But the configurations of tile patterns alone is not the only source of visual interest. The surface design on individual tiles can be as alluring and arresting, and it is here that contemporary craftsmen have brought the newest spirit to an age-old craft. Craftsmen who make, paint, or glaze their tiles by hand have been generous in introducing brilliant surface color, texture, and pattern to architectural ceramics. One-of-a-kind handmade tiles also play with shape, which commercial tiles by nature are unable to do. The spontaneous, expressionist graphics, unique applications of color and pattern, and vigorous, textured mosaics of many contemporary handmade tile installations all bring to our feet vibrant design possibilities that have traditionally remained on the wall.

Until recently, glazed tiles — which offer a nearly infinite variety of colors, textures, and surfaces — were suitable only for wall applications. But new technology has produced glazes with greater resistance. The growing availability of abrasion-resistant glazed tiles that are able to withstand continuous pressure and use on the floor has brought greater color and pattern underfoot. With it has come greater delicacy and refinement in design, in both handmade and commercial tiles. The rate of a particular tile's resistance, in relation to the traffic it is meant to absorb, should be considered in selecting floor tile. For low-traffic areas, nearly any tile may be used, although glazed tiles should have at least a low resistance to abrasion. On high-traffic areas, such as hallways, kitchens, and living areas, only glazed tiles with high abrasion resistance, and unglazed tiles, should be used.

Unglazed tiles — red stoneware, terra-cotta, and porcelain tile, to name a few — range in natural earth tones from muted taupes and grays to deeper reds and browns that impart a kind of rustic

This inventively tiled room, left, is accented by the unusual patterns of the floor and the even more surprising tile-covered table. All of the tiles were made by Starbuck Goldner Studios.

The tiles on the opposite page were created in patterns ranging from abstract petals, waves, pinwheels and pentagons to entire mosaics in a range of colors and glazes. The tiles were all handmade by Starbuck Goldner Studios.

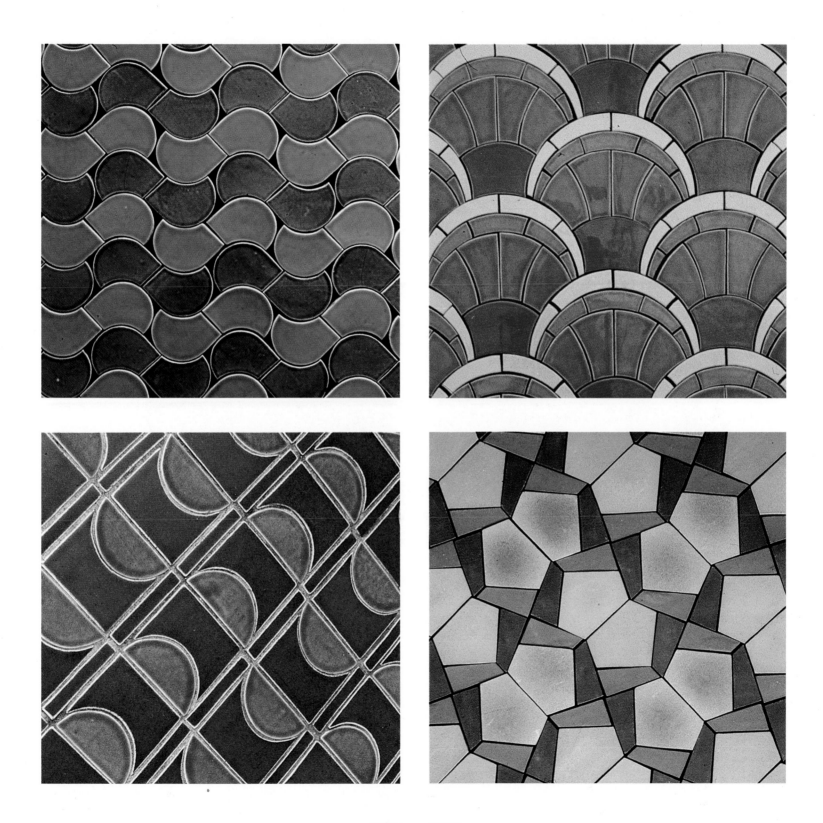

atmosphere. Their neutral tones offer countless variations and render them ideal flooring material for interiors that have an excess of patterns and color elsewhere. Their rugged physical properties permit them to withstand most of the rigors they receive underfoot. Because they also tend to be more slip-resistant than glazed tiles, unglazed tiles are often suitable for installation near outdoor areas where wetness can be tracked inside. An abrasive grit can be added to the surface of many kinds of glazed and unglazed tiles to increase their ability to guard against slipping.

The two most common means of installing floor tiles are thick-bed and thin-set installations. With the first, which is structurally stronger, the tile is applied to the existing surface with a bed of cement mortar that is anywhere from ¾ to 1¼ inch thick. Thick-bed installations, while raising the floor level slightly, also level older, worn

surfaces that may have settled into angles. They can be used to precisely define slopes or planes on the finished tile surface. Tiles applied in thin-set installations are bonded to the existing surface — which must be level and plumb — with a thinner bed of mortar. With a thinner profile and less weight, these installations can be used for wood floors that are incapable of supporting the weight of a thick-bed installation. Either method of installation is long-lasting and appropriate for the concrete or wood surfaces of most residential floors.

The fact that vibrant-patterned landscapes can lie at our feet with the same grace and ease enjoyed previously only by more rustic unglazed tiles demonstrates the increasing adaptability of the tile surface; and perhaps this also suggests that the practicality of ceramic tile as a flooring material *can* be matched by its decorative capacities.

Two-colored tile in the entrance to this second-floor living room, opposite page, creates a more elegant effect than that usually associated with this material. Using commercial tile, Alan Buchsbaum has designed a pattern that is warm and inviting.

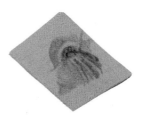

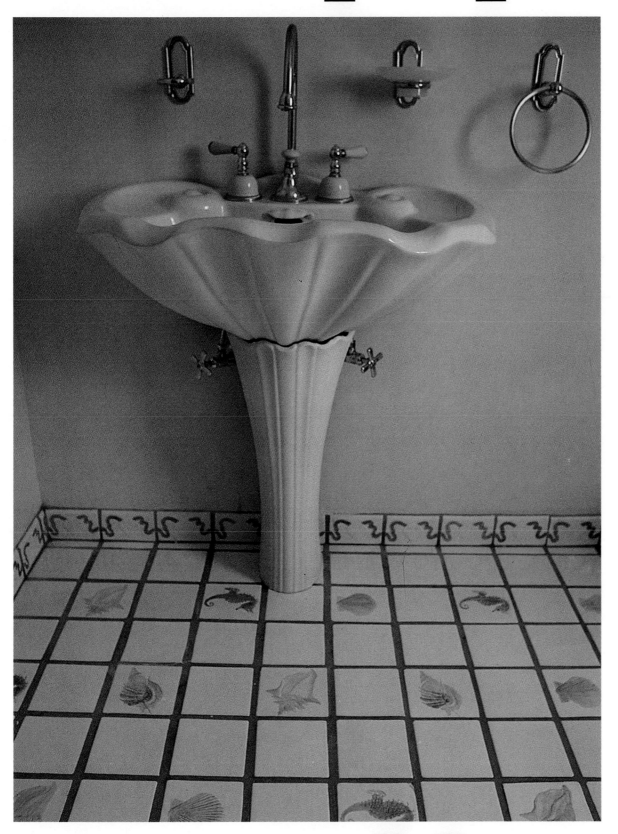

Marine imagery in watery, pastel colors was used for this bathroom floor, left. The pattern alternates simple, handmade tiles with abstract border graphics. The tiles are by Firebird Handmade Tiles.

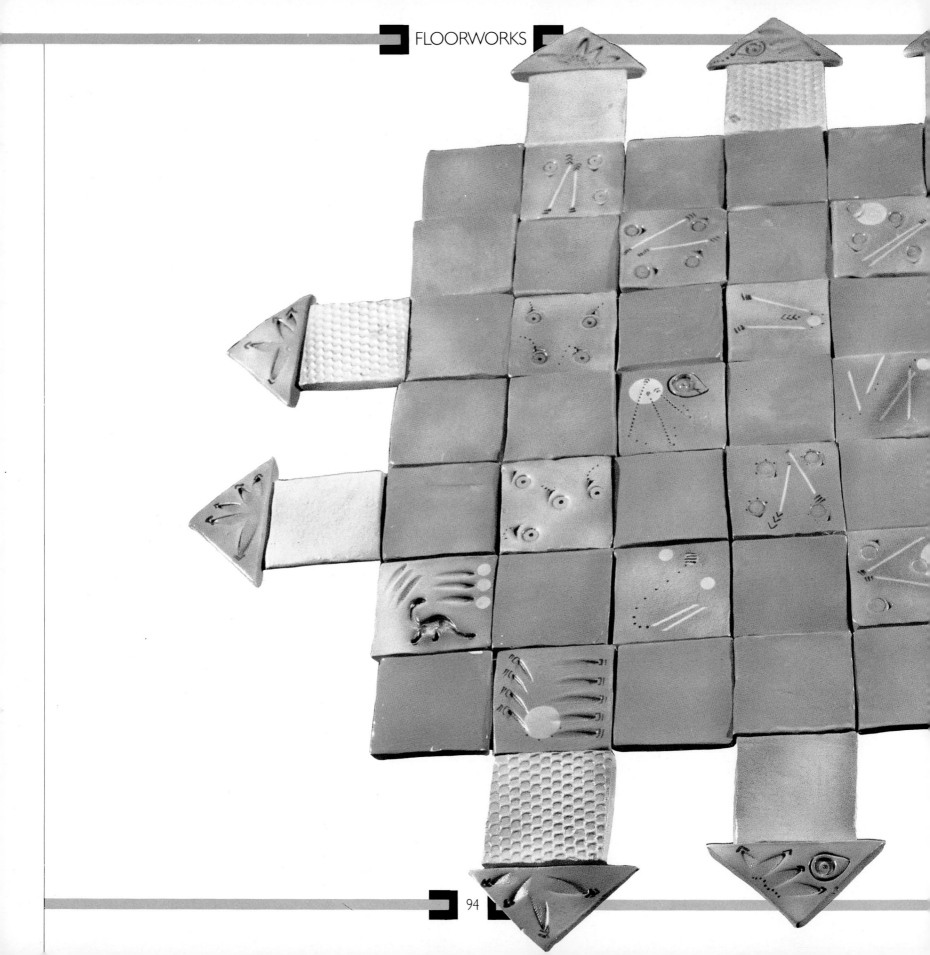

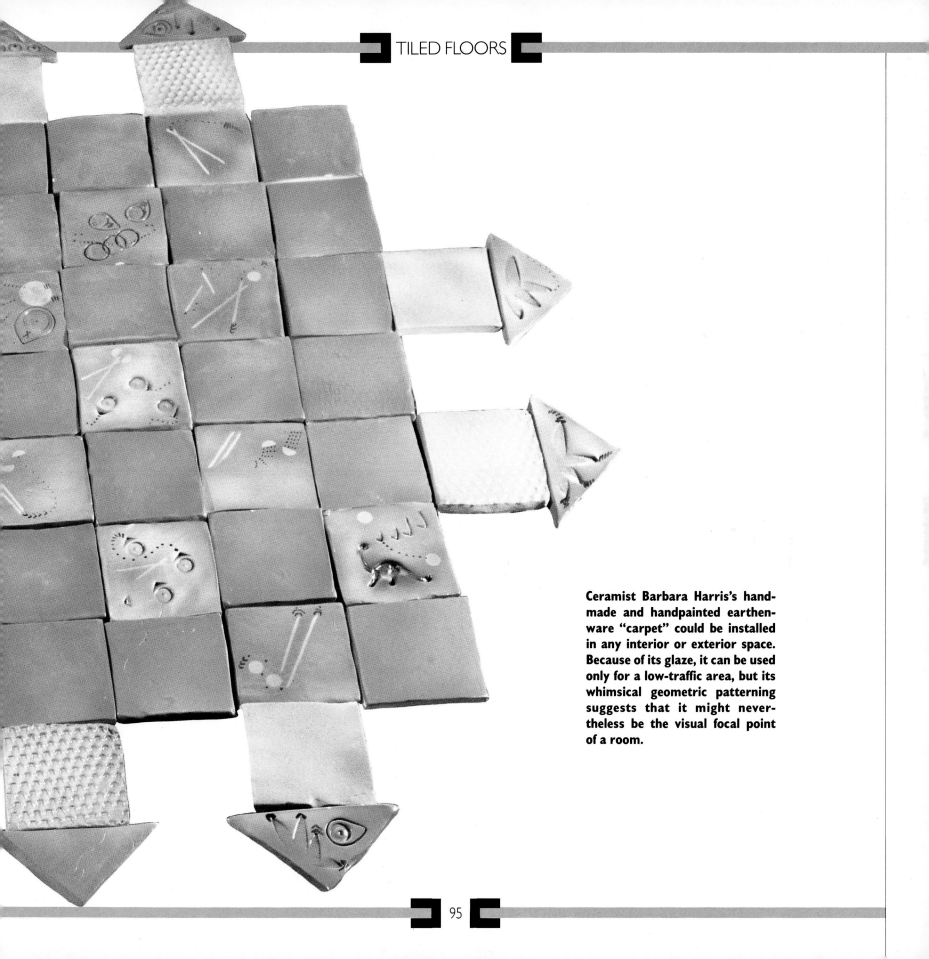

Ceramist Barbara Harris's hand-made and handpainted earthen-ware "carpet" could be installed in any interior or exterior space. Because of its glaze, it can be used only for a low-traffic area, but its whimsical geometric patterning suggests that it might never-theless be the visual focal point of a room.

CHAPTER
7
RUGS

Sisal, a fiber from the Yucatan, was used for
the floor of this beachhouse. The rough,
nubby texture of the material conveys a raw,
natural feeling that is conducive to informal
living areas such as this, proving that there is
a suitable rug for every environment. The
natural tones of the hemp also pull together
the disparate patterns and color used
elsewhere in the interior. The floor treatment
was designed by Sam Botero.

The lustrous emerald-green hearth rug designed by architect Alan Buchsbaum and produced by V'Soske subtly conforms to the outline of the hearth. Its long, narrow shape invites one to recline. Made of silk and wool, the color and texture of the rug changes when viewed from different angles. Its soft, irregular edges soften the rigid geometries of the hearth and mantle.

The tradition of using woven textiles for floorcoverings is among the most ancient in the decorative arts. The oldest rug in existence, dating back to 300 B.C. and residing now in the Hermitage Museum in Leningrad, is the Pazyryk. It was discovered in a cave in Siberia, where it had been preserved in ice for over two thousand years. Pictorial records from ancient Egypt suggest that about 3000 B.C. patterned fabrics were laid down in front of pharoahs' thrones for the comfort of royal persons. Throughout the ages textiles served multiple duties, working as tents, wallhangings, partitions, bedcovers, and in ancient Persia, even camel saddles.

The history of the rug in this country really only began in the mid-eighteenth century. Prior to that, most floors remained bare because textiles were imported and were too costly to be subjected to the rigors met underfoot. In fact, the term "rugg" referred to the bedrug used to cover the bed and other pieces of furniture for both warmth and decoration. By the middle and end of the eighteenth century, oriental rugs and carpets were being imported to the colonies in greater supply, and to protect them, smaller rugs were sewn with a two-ply yarn on a base of homespun linen. Shirred rugs, made from scraps of cloth that were more readily available than yarn, followed, as did woven and braided rugs, all of which were soon used as hearth rugs. Popular motifs tended to be patriotic, with ships, eagles, and stars. There were also narrative designs featuring farm animals, houses, people, and flowers.

The tortoise Lino Rug by A2Z is a permanently installed "area rug" constructed entirely of vintage linoleum tiles.

This Lino Rug, left, made with solid vinyl tiles inlaid on rigid panels, was created to act as an area rug. The vivid colors and strong geometric patterning recall Navajo woven rugs, but this rug is clearly a more high-tech approach, serving as a durable and easy-to-clean mat for entryways or in the kitchen or bath. Designed by A2Z, the rug can be put over carpet, wood, or tile, or can be inlaid with other flooring material.

The Task System rug, right, designed by Henry Smith-Miller and Laurie Hawkinson for V'Soske is made up of smaller rugs with subtle variations in color and texture that can be moved around. Various yarn weights, pile heights, densities, tufting directions, and shearing techniques play with texture and light in myriad patterns. The combinations of squares accommodate changing needs.

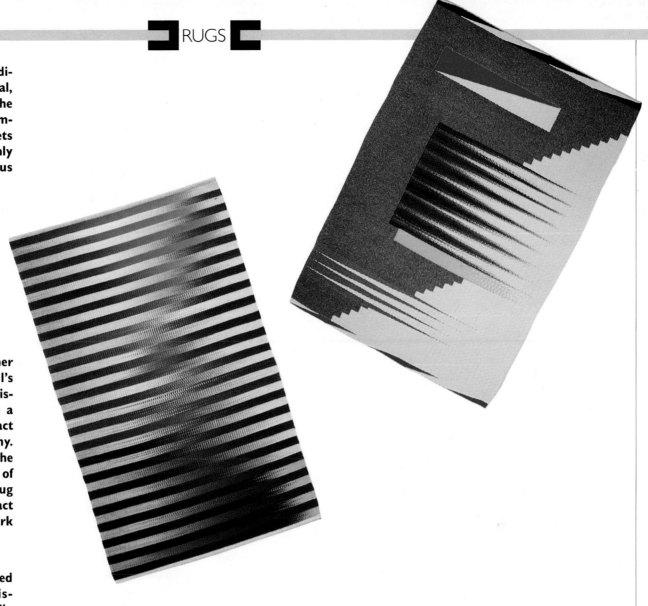

The rich landscapes created by traditional Oriental rugs remain classical, conservative surfaces that please the eye, left. Timeless, elegant, and complex in color and design, these carpets are often at their best against highly polished wood floors and lustrous wood paneling.

Gradations of cool blues and warmer browns merge in Emily Mitchell's woven wool rug, near right. Commissioned by a law office situated on a freshwater bay, the rug is an abstract representation of the local geography. The gradations in the colors of the stripes coincide into a soft river of color. While the geometry of the rug may appear traditional, the inexact and subtle patterning is indeed a mark of contemporary design.

Lively geometric patterning coupled with strong, primary colors distinguish an area rug woven by Emily Mitchell, far right. Though the colors and geometrics are based in tradition, the lack of symmetry in the piece is purely contemporary.

Because the decorative arts represent and reflect the culture from which they emerge, contemporary rugs naturally feature motifs and imagery of the contemporary world. While rugs continue to be, above all, utilitarian objects, their design has not escaped the examination and subsequent innovation that has occurred elsewhere in the textile arts. In recent years, fiber arts of all sorts have come off the loom, off the wall and floor, often to become freestanding sculptural objects in themselves. Because rugs have a practical use on the floor, however, they have not made these more exotic forays. But their patterning, texture, and decoration reflect, even if in subtle and restrained ways, a contemporary sensibility. Abstract, geometric imagery abounds. Likewise, patterns and grids are loosely established only to be broken in haphazard and seemingly random design schemes that in the end *do* adhere to some visual logic all their own. Whether these are rendered in a postmodern pastel palette or in brighter, stronger, primary colors, the spontaneity and richness in color and texture often suggest that these rugs are actually paintings in fiber.

Whether it is in commercially produced carpets or handmade rugs, eclecticism and divergence in material are often present in

Bonnie Briton's one-of-a-kind or limited edition wool rug combines precise geometric graphics with looser, more fluid images, symbols, and patterns. The result is a rich diversity that is very contemporary.

The soft gradations of color in Mary Kaspar's wool rug, opposite page, have been achieved with over thirty-five hand-dyed colors. The subtlety of tone and the softness of the surface is as suitable hanging on the wall as it is lying flat on the floor.

The graphics on three rugs designed by Steven Holl for a New York City apartment, right, correspond to the architectural motifs found elsewhere in the apartment. The living area is such a vast space that the imagery on the rug has a loose, spatial feeling to it. The drafting table in the den suggests planes, an impression reinforced by the flat images floating across the rug. And the thin tubing of the table in the dining area is echoed by textured line drawings underfoot. All in all, the series demonstrates that provocative and arresting design on the floor does not interfere with that of the room, but instead may reinforce it with wit and elegance.

contemporary work. The *combined* uses of materials also distinguish many rugs made today. Densely tufted, contoured silk and worsted wool may be used in a single piece, with their varying textures and sheen capturing the light as different pigments might on canvas. Or, various yarn weights, pile heights, densities, shearing techniques, and tufting directions could all make for divergent textures on a rug of a single color. Add variations in color as well, and the surface interest in these pieces becomes all the more intense. In handmade rugs, some pieces combine hooking — the process of forcing loops of yarn or narrow strips of rag through a pre-woven backing to create a pile — with straight fabric or have had paints and dyes applied directly to the woven surface. Rag rugs can be paint-splashed and also quilted or lightly stuffed with old-fashioned borders. Often, such a play with material will dictate or otherwise affect the exterior shape of the rug. The conventional forms — square, rectangular, circular, or oval — no

longer necessarily define a rug's form.

Rugs serve a number of practical functions as well. Although contemporary rugs may not necessarily serve as many practical purposes as their predecessors, they do still address multiple needs. They bring warmth and comfort under foot. The acoustical advantages of rugs is that they soften and muffle sound more effectively than any other surfacing material for the floor and thus are especially suited to high-traffic areas. Rugs also offer safety for slippery, high-gloss surfaces. Finally, they reduce wear to the floor.

The tradition of laying rugs at our feet was established countless generations ago, and it is continued today in altogether modern treatments that not only reflect a contemporary aesthetic, but also the technological achievements of materials and construction made in recent years. The splendor and diversity apparent in these pieces are testimony to the art, craft, and industry in the textile arts.

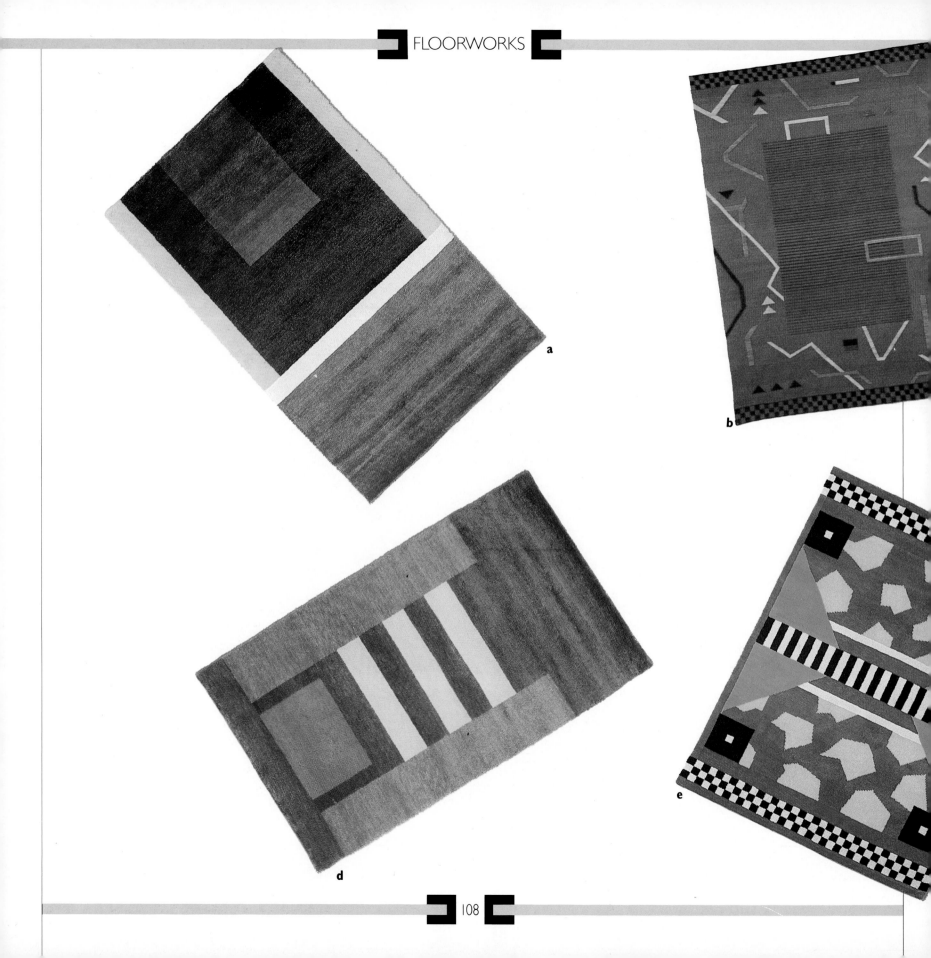

a

b

d

e

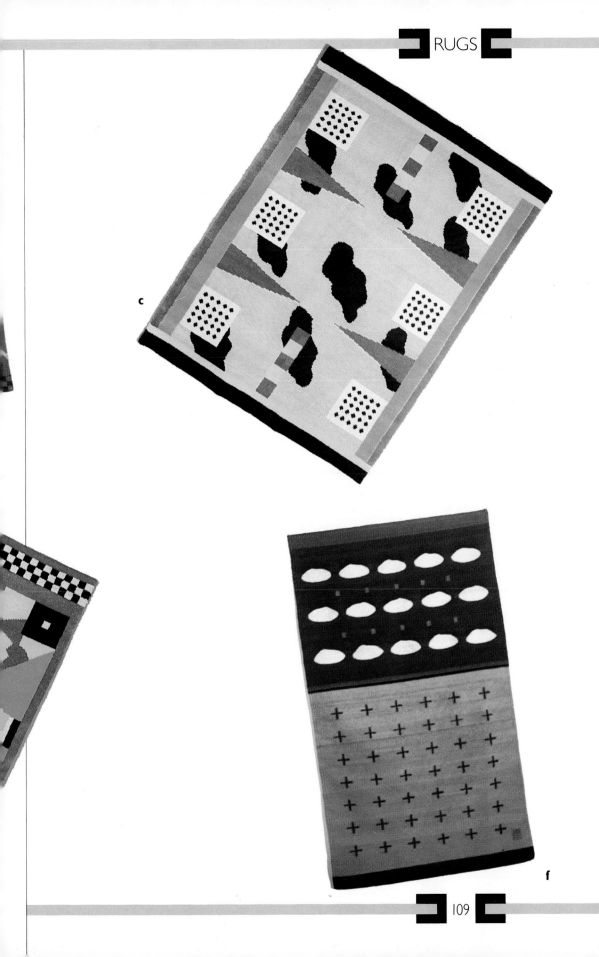

c

f

The Memphis Milano limited editions of rugs reflect the Italian design collective's commitment to innovative applications of color and form. The rugs are named after American states: (b) Arizona (c) Tennessee (d) California (f) Oregon. Bright blocks of colors and the coupling of strict pattern with random imagery reflects a rampant post-modern style that so distinguished Memphis in its early days. But these rugs are handwoven wool, and entirely functional, distinguishing them from the intellectual and aesthetic pranks found elsewhere in the Memphis collection. Bonnie Briton's one-of-a-kind wool rugs, (a) and (e), also combine precise geometric graphics with loose images. The result is an appealingly contemporary look.

This carpet, right, has been put to innovative use on a dining room table. The neutral color of the flooring material is enlivened by the design of the carpet.

A rug by Carolyn Bowler, left, was handwoven with felted wool strips. A felt ball looks as though it has surfaced from a flat ground of textile, bringing the rug into the realm of sculpture. Though this foray into the three-dimensional is obviously atypical in traditional rug design and construction, the subdued colors, materials, and restrained patterns used are traditional, making for an even more surprising effect.

CHAPTER
8
FLOORCLOTHS

The oval floorcloth designed and painted by
Lynn Goodpasture is the perfect focal point
for the oval hallways of a New York City
residence. The stone and marble pattern was
painted to evoke a garden courtyard that
contains blocks of gray and white stone,
precious stone inlays, and diamond-shaped
marble inlays.

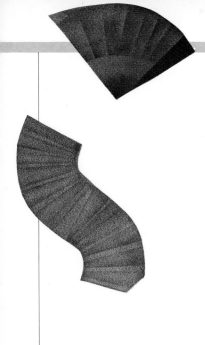

The fans on a floorcloth by Lynn Goodpasture were stenciled and handpainted randomly across the surface of the canvas in deep, intense colors. Backed with felt and protected with three coats of polyurethane, the floorcloth is extremely durable.

In early American decorative arts, painted floorcloths were nearly as common as painted and stenciled floors. Durable cloth, usually sailcloth imported from England, was handpainted, stenciled, and used as a surrogate for costlier woven rugs and carpets. Like stenciled and painted floors, painted floorcloths were easily refinished, repainted, and patched when frayed and worn. The added advantage to floorcloths was their portability. They could be easily moved from room to room, or from home to home.

The appeal of floorcloths has been rejuvenated today, although the designs on the painted canvas are more contemporary both in design and use of color. Because the floorcloth is painted canvas, it is a direct relation to painted canvases of the fine arts. But the connection is not simply a material one; often, the vibrant color and pattern applied to canvas reflect a sensibility with roots in the fine arts. Many surfaces, for example, have been textured and spattered with expressionist spontaneity. Or, contemporary cloths often have architectural themes and fantasy finishes that abound elsewhere in the decorative arts. Just as earlier floorcloths featured themes of their time — patriotic, nautical, floral, or domestic — contemporary cloths also reflect the culture from which they emerge.

The intricate patterns of the basket that is the focal point of this floorcloth by Lynn Goodpasture give the entire piece the look of a painting.

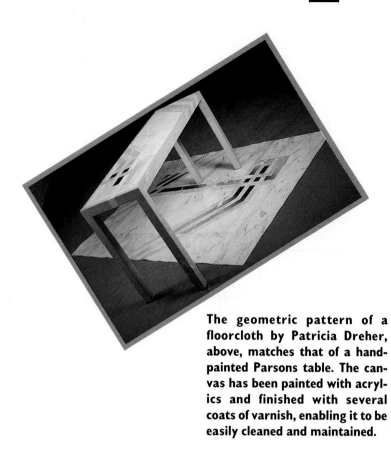

The geometric pattern of a floorcloth by Patricia Dreher, above, matches that of a hand-painted Parsons table. The canvas has been painted with acrylics and finished with several coats of varnish, enabling it to be easily cleaned and maintained.

The pattern of this floorcloth by Patricia Dreher has an architectural quality; the final effect is reminiscent of architectural drawings. The subdued, pastel palette softens the strong lines. Acrylic paints and varnish form a long-lasting surface.

The stylized seashell medallion floorcloth was designed by Dennis Abbe and painted by artisans of Evergreene Painting Studios. The fantasy marble finish is in a deep red unlike any found in nature, and is framed in gold leaf trim. Painted in oil and finished with numerous layers of varnish, each of which has been sanded, the floorcloth can withstand the rigors it will receive underfoot in a hallway.

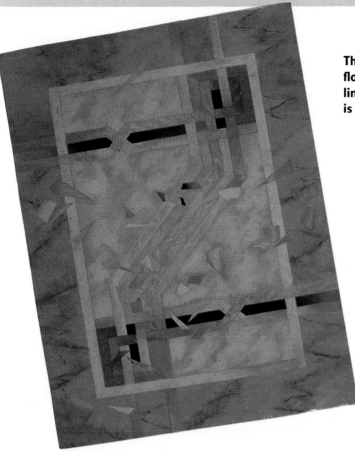

The subdued, pastel palette of this floorcloth, left, softens the strong lines of its patterns. The floorcloth is by Patricia Dreher.

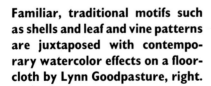

Familiar, traditional motifs such as shells and leaf and vine patterns are juxtaposed with contemporary watercolor effects on a floorcloth by Lynn Goodpasture, right.

Contemporary materials — durable acrylic paints, sturdy polyurethane and acrylic finishes and varnishes — tend to make contemporary floorcloths more practical than their predecessors. Four or five coats of polyurethane make the cloth easier to clean with soap and water and give it a sleek, wet look that becomes glossier when bright, vibrant colors are used. And, contrary to popular belief, floorcloths *are* suited to medium and high-traffic areas. The weight of the finishes helps to keep the fabric flat on the floor, and tape on the underside of the cloth, or tacks, can be used if necessary. Floorcloths can be backed with a felt lining, although this may result in a "spongy" surface.

Floorcloths work best on surfaces of wood, tile, linoleum, or concrete, but when placed on top of carpeting, traffic stress is usually too great. They can be cut or hemmed, or the canvas can be fringed as a playful reference to woven area rugs. With several coats of varnish to protect the painted surface, floorcloths continue to enjoy the advantages of both the rug and painted floor. Stiff, smooth, shiny, and brightly colored, they function as linoleum rugs and are as easily maintained. Like rugs, the heavy fabric brings warmth, quiet, and is safe to walk on. And like rugs, floorcloths reduce wear to the floor. On the other hand, the smooth, glossy surfaces and the design, color, and patterning that can be achieved by painting canvas are entirely different from those of woven or tufted rugs and carpets. Both decorative and practical floor surfaces, floorcloths use the best of several different mediums.

A lively parade of hens and chickens obligingly follow a rooster around the border of a floorcloth designed by Virginia Crawford for a Long Island kitchen, below. The interior of the floorcloth was sponged over a layer of actual chicken wire for a positive/negative surface effect, while the chickens themselves were stenciled on canvas. Although the heavy canvas does not have any backing, it sits flat on the floor with an acrylic undercoat, acrylic paint, and three coats of a varethane finish.

Bee Morrow and Randy Jones of Decorative Arts Limited scattered a floral design across this floorcloth, left, which measures approximately 10 by 15 feet. Its pink border gives shape to the room, while its pastel tones take their cue from furnishings in the room. The floorcloth was made from heavy-grade commercial canvas duck cloth, acrylic paints, and several coats of polyurethane.

Designed and painted by Jeff Greene of Ever-greene Painting Studios, this floorcloth com-bines a geometric maze against a fantasy marble background. What is unusual about this floorcloth is the fringe that hangs from one side, a whimsical reminder that this is an area rug. Oil paints and varnish permit the floor-cloth to endure heavy traffic.

Faux marble columns supporting a glass top dining table themselves rest on a trompe l'oleil floorcloth. The cloth is a faux sandstone with a mosaic border based on a Pompeiin motif. The entire faux scene was designed and painted by Tromploy.

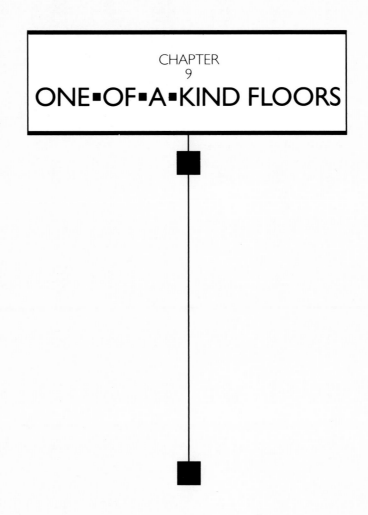

CHAPTER
9
ONE·OF·A·KIND FLOORS

*This scintillating floor, created with
completely unconventional materials, is a
stunning example of what can happen when
traditional design rules are broken.*

Like the walls above it, the floor of this Santa Fe house has been constructed of adobe. The ceiling, on the other hand, is wood. By reversing the traditional placement of materials, designers Rena and Ralph Swentzel have found an original design solution. A dark glaze was applied to the adobe to both protect it and to create a design that would look like oversize ceramic floor tiles.

Unique applications of paint, stains, tiles, textiles, exotic woods, and genuine and faux stones create many of the floors shown in this book. By definition and by nature, many of these are one-of-a-kind, true originals. Yet there are floors that go even further. These design departures are made with unusual materials or ordinary materials in unusual combinations; the design may be approached in a completely unconventional manner; or unexpected elements are introduced to challenge our notion of what a floor should be.

The joining of different and seemingly disparate materials make many of these floor treatments surprising. A surface as ancient and basic as tile is made new again with the addition of marble to make a wild mosaic, or is inlaid in carpeting to meld the contemporary with the traditional. In the case of a studio floor designed by architect Charles Jencks, the mix of materials is the more abstract interplay of light with painted wood, as sunlight hits the floor at different times of day and creates various patterns.

Not only does innovation with materials create one-of-a-kind floors, but creative applications of those materials sometimes make for an entirely new look. The process can be as interesting as the

Ceramic tiles do not necessarily have anything to do with the repetition of image, shape, or color. This is conveyed clearly and colorfully by Phillip Maberry's tile and marble mosaic floor, left. Brilliantly colored, irregularly shaped ceramic tiles visually collide with shards of real marble, making an explosive surface pattern.

The precision cut of this carpet in an entry hall melds it with the checkerboard floor tiles of the adjacent office area, opposite page. The austere gray of the carpet is livened up with this sawtooth border, which also serves to visually separate the two areas. The entire area was designed by Space Inceptions.

Conrad Malicoat used recycled bricks in a one-of-a-kind design for a foyer floor, right, cutting some of the bricks by hand into smaller fragments to create the leaping fish motif.

The painted floors of this studio in the woods of Cape Cod are a subtle reminder of the slats, beams, and railings found elsewhere in the architecture of the cottage. The shades of blue seem to reflect the ocean, sky, and ponds of the local landscape. The light and shadow created by the slats of the studio's rotunda fall across the painted stripes of the floor and act as a kind of sundial, telling the time of day by the position of the patterns that shift as the light shifts. It is this continual interplay of color and light that makes this floor truly one-of-a-kind.

The shimmering aquamarine floor created for a New York City loft explores new frontiers in floor design. The poured concrete floor was polished and smoothed so that the chips of stone aggregate which naturally appear in concrete acquired a new surface luster. Polyurethane, thinned to a water-like consistency, was then mixed with dry aquamarine pigment and applied to seal the floor surface. Layers of additional pigment mixed with denatured alcohol were then added. This entire process was then repeated five or six times, and the floor was finally buffed with a clear wax. The iridescence of the cobalt surface is due not simply to the pigment, but to the shimmer of eye shadows and powders that were mixed in as well at the suggestion of Rick Gillete, a makeup artist who designed the floor with Franklin D. Israel. Yet despite the layers of materials, the texture of the concrete remains. And since parts of the concrete base were poured later than others, there was a variance in the way the old and new areas of the floor absorbed the pigment, making for even greater depth and texture.

finished floor itself. The shimmering floor in Rick Gillete's New York City loft was created by applying layers of shimmering cobalt pigment that had been thinned with polyurethane to smoothed concrete. The iridescence itself was created by mixing cosmetic eye shadows with paints. The polished concrete, the combined use of pigment and polyurethane, and, of course, the makeup create a surface that has no precedent either in materials or process.

Trickery is not only employed in the ancient art of faux and trompe l'oeil finishes, but also in brand new creative applications. In a Sante Fe house, an entire room is turned around by a floor made of adobe, and a ceiling made of wood. The floor, however, is glazed and ruled off to look like giant ceramic tiles, further challenging the viewer's perceptions.

Just as innovative are those handcrafted surfaces that are unique in their expressions of a personal and private imagery. Ceramist Conrad Malicoat's leaping fish made from recycled brick for an entryway is an excellent example of a personal vision brought to life. Some surfaces, such as the tile and marble mosaic by Phillip Maberry, are lively expressionist graphics that might more typically be found hanging as art on the wall, rather than appearing on the floor that one is expected to step across.

The vibrant textures and hues found on these floors, the surprising and unexpected designs, and the use and combination of unlikely materials suggest that these surfaces are setting the stage for some exotic performance. Yet it is the floors themselves that are the grandest productions, providing entertainment, delight, and a sense of being brought into a world of creativity and craft.

APPENDIX

SOURCES

AMERICAN

ARCHITECTS AND DESIGNERS

DENNIS ABBE
246 West End Avenue
New York, NY 10023
212■787■3851

BOOTH-HANSEN & ASSOCIATES
555 South Dearborn
Chicago, Il 60605
312■427■0300

SAM BOTERO, ASSOCIATES
150 East 58 Street
New York, NY 10155
212■935■5155

ALAN BUSHSBAUM
℅ Anderson/Schwartz
40 Hudson Street
New York, NY 10013
212■608■0185

NICHOLAS A. CALDER LIMITED
348 East 58th Street
New York, NY 10022
212■861■9055

DOROTHY DAVIS
Davis Tile Techniques
827 Exposition Avenue
Dallas, TX 75226
214■826■5130

DECORATIVE ARTS LIMITED
2137 W. Alabama
Houston, TX 77098
713■520■1680

DAVID EASTON
323 East 58 Street
New York, NY 10022
212■486■6704

HARIET ECKSTEIN
One Fifth Avenue
New York, NY 10003
212■475■0045

RONN JAFFE ASSOCIATES, INC.
9204 Harrington
Potomac, MA 20854
301■365■3500

MICHAEL GRAVES
341 Nassau Street
Princeton, NJ 08540
609■924■6409

STEVEN HOLL
435 Hudson Street
New York, NY 10014
212■989■0918

RICHARD KNAPPLE
V.P. Interior Design
Bloomingdale's
1000 Third Avenue
New York, NY 10022
212■705■2592

OKG ARCHITECTS
Oliver, Kurze, Georges
1053 N. Michigan Ave.
Pasadena, CA 91104
818■398■8346

NANCY M. POPE
83 Pinckney Street
Boston, MA 02114
617■227■5006

HENRY SMITH-MILLER
305 Canal Street
New York, NY 10013
212■996■3875

WOOD

DESIGNED WOOD FLOORING CENTER
281 Lafayette Street
New York, NY 10012
212■925■6633

KENTUCKY WOOD FLOORS
P.O. Box 33276
Louisville, KY 40232
502■451■6024

YOST & COMPANY
2212 Woodhead
Houston, TX 77019
713■526■3434

PAINTINGS AND SURFACE FINISH STUDIOS

THE DAY STUDIO WORKSHOP, INC.
1504 Bryant Street
San Francisco, CA 94103
415■626■9300

EVERGREENE PAINTING STUDIOS, INC.
635 West 23 Street
New York, NY 10011
212■727■9500

RICHARD GILLETTE & STEVEN SHADLEY
144 West 27th Street
New York, NY 10001
212■243■6913

POLLY LEWIS
3 Cherrywood
Locust Valley, NY 11560
516■674■3538

THOMAS MELVIN PAINTING STUDIO
2860 West Leland Avenue
Chicago, IL 60625
312■588■2932

RINDER'S NEW YORK FLOORING
129 East 124 Street
New York, NY 10035
212■427■6262

SERPENTINE STUDIO LIMITED
435 Greenwich Street
New York, NY 10013
212■925■7610

MICHAEL THORNTON-SMITH
123 Chambers Street
New York, NY 10007
212■619■5338

TROMPLOY, INC.
119 West 25th Street
New York, NY 10011
212■366■5579

STENCILS

LARRY BOYCE & ASSOCIATES, INC.
Box 421507
San Francisco, CA 94142
415■626■2122

VIRGINIA CRAWFORD
285 West Broadway
Studio 310
New York, NY 10013
212■226■6259

DECORATIVE ARTS LIMITED
2011 South Shepherd
Houston, TX 77019
713■520■1680

EVERGREENE PAINTING STUDIOS, INC.
635 West 23 Street
New York, NY 10011
212■727■9500

LYNN GOODPASTURE
42 West 17 Street
New York, NY 10003
212■645■5334

CILE LORD
42 East 12 Street
New York, NY 10003
212■757■2774

LESLIE ANN POWERS
241 State Street
Guildford, CT 06487
203■453■9853

LAURA TORBET STUDIO
225 East 73 Street
New York, NY 10021
212■988■2898

TILES

FIREBIRD, INC.
4 Spring Street
Morristown, NJ 07960
201■267■0414

DOROTHY HAFNER
44 Cooper Square
New York, NY 10003
212■677■9797

BARBARA HARRIS
P.O. Box 385
Walker Valley, NY 12588
914■647■3817

ITALIAN TILE CENTER
499 Park Avenue
New York, NY 10022
212■226■4375

PHILIP MABERRY
767 South Street
Highland, NY 12528
914■883■5032

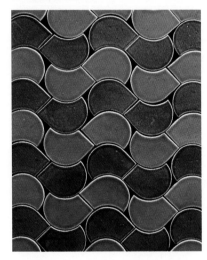

STARBUCK GOLDNER STUDIO
315 West 4 Street
Bethlehem, PA 18015
215■866■6321

CONRAD MALICOAT
Brick Breakthroughs
312 Bradford St.
Provincetown, MA 02657
508■487■0214

RUGS

A2Z
Box 351389
Los Angeles, CA 90035
213■937■2072

CAROLYN S. BOWLER
101 South Almon #1
Moscow, ID 83843
208■882■7006

**MEMPHIS MILANO
ARTEMIDE INC.**
150 East 58th Street
New York, NY 10155
212■980■0710

EMILY MITCHELL
3716 Jefferson
Traverse City, MI 49694
616■946■1989

V'SOSKE
155 East 56 Street
New York, NY 10022
212■688■1150

FLOORCLOTHS

VIRGINIA CRAWFORD
285 West Broadway
Studio 310
New York, NY 10013
212■226■6259

PATRICIA DREHER
247 Mississippi Street
San Francisco, CA 94107
415■626■0621

**EVERGREENE PAINTING
STUDIOS, INC.**
635 West 23 Street
New York, NY 10011
212■727■9500

LYNN GOODPASTURE
42 West 17 Street
New York, NY 10011
212■645■5334

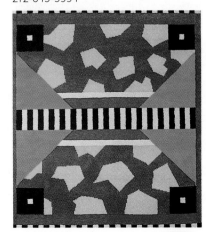

BRITISH

WOOD

GC FLOORING & FURNISHING LTD
George House, Unit 3
Perivale Industrial Park
Perivale
Middlesex UB6 7RL
081■991 1000

LASSCO TIMBER LTD
Mark Street (off Paul Street)
London EC2A 4ER
071■729 3620

STANDARD FLOORING LTD
6 South Hill Park
London NW3
071■435 6998

PAINTERS AND SURFACE FINISH STUDIOS

CHRISTOPHER BOULTER
43 Goodrich Road
London SE22
071■299 2219

CLASSIC GROUP
153 Westbourne Grove
London W11
071■221 6365

DECARTE
268 Gloucester Terrace
London W2 6HU
071■727 8294

LAURA JEFFREYS
29 Brunswick Gardens
London W8 4AW
071■727 9517

NICHOLAS LLEWELLYN DECORATION
27 Klea Avenue
London SW4
071■673 2072

GEORGE MORRIS
22 Fair Tree Road
Epsom Downs
Surrey
07373 59558

MONICA PITMAN ASSOCIATES
20 Courtfield Gardens
London SW7
071■370 6655

JAYNE SIMCOCK
29 St Margaret's Grove
Twickenham
Middlesex TW1 1JF
081■892 9238

STENCILERS

ANDREW BRADLEY
24 Kensington Gardens
Camden
Bath BA1 6LH
0225 317025

SUSIE GRADWELL STENCILS
1 The Old Bakery
Long Street, Croscombe
Near Wells
Somerset
0749 2429

HAND PAINTED STENCILS
6 Polestead Road
Oxford OX2 6TW
0865 56072

LYN LE GRICE STENCIL DESIGNS
Alsia Mill
St. Buryan
Cornwall
0736 72765

CAROLYN WARRENDER
1 Ellis Street
London SW1
071■730 0728

TILES

CORNWISE LTD
168 Old Brompton Road
London SW5
071■373 6890

ELON TILES
8 Clarendon Cross
Holland Park
London W11
071■727 0884

L.R. CERAMICS
The Pavement
Popes Lane
London W5
071■579 7190

WORLD'S END TILES
British Rail Yard
Silverthorne Road
London SW8
071■720 8358

CANADIAN

PAINTERS AND SURFACE FINISH STUDIOS

LA BOITE DU PINCEAU D'ARLEQUIN
760, rue St. Felix
Montréal, PQ H3L 2B8
514■878■9166

COLLECTORS CUSTOM FURNITURE
8920 Shaunessey Street
Vancouver, BC V6P 3Y5
604■321■5171

FAMOUS PAINTERS
5785 Victoria Drive
Vancouver, BC V5P 3W5
604■324■1923

FINE ARTISTS AT WORK
#1A–1215 13th Street SE
Calgary, AB T2G 3J4
403■263■2877

FREESTYLE DECORATIVE FINISHES
% 4945 Lochside Drive
Victoria, BC V8Y 2E6
604■385■8131

RICHARD GORDON ENTERPRISES
174 Neville Park Blvd.
Toronto, ON M4E 3P8
416■690■2644

LAPRES & LAPRES
#3–2256 West 3rd Avenue
Vancouver, BC V6K 1M1
604■736■1150

MASTER HAND PAINTING & DECORATING
321 John Street
Nanaimo, BC V9S 5K1
604■753■0016

MARIO NOVIELLO
#3–7 Fraser Avenue
Toronto, ON M6K 1Y9
416■531■5328

WESTERN WALLPRINTING
#4–7419 50th Avenue
Calgary, AB T4P 1M5
403■236■4559

WOOD ART PRODUCTS
70 Snidecrost Road, Unit M
Toronto, ON L4K 2K3
416■660■3839

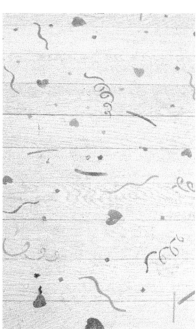

TILES AND MARBLE

CERAMATILE LTD.
383 Chenton Avenue
Winnipeg, MB R3G 0H3
204■339■0217

COUNTRY TILES
321 Davenport Road
Toronto, ON M5R 1K5
416■922■9214

DRIMO TILE
102–333 Terminal
Vancouver, BC V6A 2L7
604■687■8453

NEW ENGLAND SLATE
P.O. Box 503
St. Catherines, ON L2R 6V9
416■892■5793

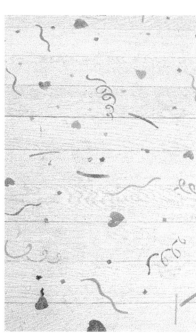

ANN SACKS TILE & STONE
2349 Granville Street
Vancouver, BC V6H 3G4
604■737■7966

TIVOLI MARBLE & CERAMIC INC.
4801 Keele Street
Downsview, ON M3J 3A4
416■667■0010

TMT MARBLE SUPPLY
900 Keele Street
Toronto, ON M6N 3E7
416■653■6111

WOOD

GENERAL WOODS & VENEERS LTD.
P.O. Box 1059, Station A
Montréal, PQ H3C 2X6
416■674■4957

HARDWOOD MILLING CO. LTD.
225 Salsbury Drive
Vancouver, BC V5L 3Y8
604■255■5767

PHOTO CREDITS

© Peter Aaron/Esto: 14-15

Courtesy of A2Z: 100, 101 top

John Babcock/Bonnie Briton: 104-105, 108 top right, 108 lower right, 109 lower right

Oberto Gili Berkey: 24 upper left, 124, 132-133

Carolyn Bowler: 110, 111

Karen Bussolini: 60-61, 62-63, 74, 75 middle, 128 lower right

Richard Champion/Samuel Botero Associates: 96

Toward Chess/Polly Lewis: 71

Sandy Cies: 94-95

Tom Collicot: 18, 19 lower right

Virginia Crawford/Virginia Design Studio: 57, 120 lower right

David Arky Photo: 56, 119 lower right

Courtesy of Day Studio Workshop, Inc.: 78

Nick Edwards/Serpentine Studio Ltd.: 38-39, 46-47, 68 lower right

George Erml: 84-84, 86 lower right

Firebird, Inc./Steven Strauss: 93

Lynn Goodpasture: 51, 52, 54, 55 lower, 114-115

Nick Grande: 72 top

Jeff Greene/Evergreene Painting Studio: 75 top, 18, 121

Linda Hackett: 112

Nancy Halverson: 75 bottom

Interior Designer/Harriet Eckstein: 59

The Italian Tile Center: 82, 86 upper left

Charles Jencks: 130-131

Courtesy of Kentucky Wood Floors: 20, 23, 24 lower right, 25, 26-27, 28-29, 30-31, 32-33, 34-35

Richard Knapple: 44-45, 48

Bill Lindhaut: 70

Kristine Larsen: 73

Courtesy of Memphis Milano Limited: 109 top

Ed Mendez © 1985 Starbuck Goldner Studio: 90

Norman McGralle: 16

Emily Mitchell: 103

Phillip Nilsson: 80, 129

Naoki Okamoto: 128 upper left

OKG Architects: 40 left & lower left

Robert Perron: 43 bottom, 50 upper left, 53, 58, 67, 83, 120 upper left, 126-127

Rinder's New York Flooring: 41, 42

Susie Romanik: 107

Mark Roskams: 76-77

Lee Seatheree: 116 top

Stephen Shadley: 66

Carmen Spera: 43 upper left

© 1985 Starbuck Goldner Studio: 91

Ezra Stoller/Esto: 22

Tim Street-Porter: 12, 19 upper left, 36, 102

Gerard Taylor: 108

Michael Thorton-Smith: 69, 72 bottom

Laura Torbet: 55 top

Tromploy Inc.: 68 upper left, 78 lower right, 122-123

Marco Antonio de Valdivia: 101 bottom

Scott Walker: 87

Paul Warchol: 17, 106

Bruce Wolf: 64

INDEX